# MANAGEMENT AND MACHIAVELLI

## DISCOVERING A NEW SCIENCE OF MANAGEMENT IN THE TIMELESS PRINCIPLES OF STATECRAFT

*Antony Jay*

Pfeiffer
& COMPANY

Amsterdam • Johannesburg • Oxford
San Diego • Sydney • Toronto

Cover Design: John Odam
Compositor: Lee Ann Hubbard
Editor: Mike Werthman

**Library of Congress Cataloging-in-Publication Data**

Jay, Antony, 1930-
  Management and Machiavelli: discovering a new science
  of management in the timeless principles of statecraft
  / Antony Jay.
    p.  cm.
  Includes bibliographical references and index.
  ISBN 0-89384-260-5 (pbk.)
  1. Organizational behavior. 2. Corporations. 3. Management
  4. State, The. 5. Machiavelli, Niccolò, 1469-1527. I. Title.
  HD58.7.J38 1994                                    94-5605
  658—dc20                                           CIP

Printed in the United States of America.

Printing  1  2  3  4  5  6  7  8  9  10

# CONTENTS

# ACKNOWLEDGMENTS

It is not possible to acknowledge all those friends and acquaintances who have furnished ideas and material for this book; but I must record my debt to Donald Baverstock, with whom I have had many discussions of management theory over the past ten years, and whose acute observations and original theories have been a constant stimulus; to Geoffrey Best, professor of modern history at Edinburgh University, for professional guidance on many occasions; to Peter Parker, Clifford Oldham, Wynford Vaughan Thomas, and the London staff of White Weld, who all read the first draft of this book and supplied valuable comments, criticism, and suggestions; and to Arthur Cohen of Holt, Rinehart and Winston and Robin Denniston of Hodder and Stoughton, for the moral and material encouragement without which the book would never have been written.

# PREFACE

This book is not, and never was intended to be, a commentary on industry and management. It is an examination of the behavior of large corporate organizations, private and public, and of the people who work in them, in political and historical rather than industrial, social, or economic terms. The names may change, but their nature does not. They all still have their kings, their barons, and their courtiers, their allies and enemies, their colonies and their praetorian guard, their periods of decline, of renaissance, and of reformation. Indeed, the corporate organization has, if anything, grown to dominate the lives of even more people—as employees, customers, or suppliers—in the final decades of the twentieth century; so the need to understand them has presumably grown too. *Management and Machiavelli* is an attempt to provide that understanding. Whether it does so is for the reader, not the writer, to say.

# INTRODUCTION

"In the modern world," wrote Bertrand Russell in *Authority and the Individual*, "and still more, so far as can be guessed, in the world of the near future, important achievement is and will be almost impossible to an individual if he cannot dominate some vast organization." Nothing has happened since those words were written in 1948 to suggest that they are in any way an overstatement: On the contrary, more and more of us have come to depend directly or indirectly on the patronage of vast organizations for our livelihood, and on their behavior for the quality of our lives.

Over the years, we have amassed a great body of knowledge about corporations. For the interested student there are innumerable figures, facts, books, papers and articles, speeches, lectures, seminars and courses, studies by accountants and systems analysts and management scientists and sociologists and stockbrokers, and endless tables of statistics. Unfortunately, our understanding has not grown alongside our knowledge. Indeed, the more facts they know, the more most people seem to despair of ever coming to a real understanding of corporations as a whole because they are made up of so many complicated parts. As the need to understand these institutions grows, so the possibility of doing so recedes.

Or rather, it seems to recede; because, in fact, there is a simple framework into which all these diverse observations fit neatly and appropriately. But it means looking at the corporations in a new way: looking not through the eyes of the accountant and systems analyst and economist and mathematician, but through those of the historian and political scientist. Just what that means, it is the purpose of this book to illustrate.

It does not attempt to supply more information about the corporations: heaven forbid. Its purpose is to make sense of the vast amount of information we already have.

> Nor do I hold with those who regard it as presumption if a man of low and humble condition dare to discuss and settle the concerns of princes; because, just as those who draw landscapes place themselves below in the plain to contemplate the nature of the mountains and of lofty places, and in order to contemplate the plains place themselves high upon the mountains, even so to understand the nature of the people it needs to be a prince, and to understand that of princes it needs to be of the people.
>
> Machiavelli, *The Prince*, Dedication

> The summits of the various kinds of business are, like the tops of mountains, much more alike than the parts below. The bare principles are much the same; it is only the rich variegated details of the lower strata that so contrast with one another. But it needs travelling to know that the summits *are* the same. Those who live on one mountain believe that *their mountain is wholly unlike all others.*
>
> Walter Bagehot, *The English Constitution*

# 1

## MANAGEMENT AND MACHIAVELLI

It must all have been so easy in the nineteenth century. You built your factory, you installed your machines, you hired your labor, and you bought your raw materials, and there you were—a full-blown manufacturer. Of course you had problems: your product had to reach a standard of performance and a competitive price, you had to get it to where people could buy it, you needed capital to expand or break into new markets. But these have always been the problems of men who make and sell; they are the framework in which the industrialist has always expected to operate and the soil in which he flourishes. He sees, or feels in his bones, something that people would pay money for if it were obtainable, he knows how he can make it at a cost that will leave him a profit margin, and he has the drive to raise the capital, build the factory, and start producing and selling. This is the primal, rudimentary urge of the entrepreneur-industrialist; the essentials have not changed throughout history, and presumably they will never change.

But today there is something else the industrialist has to master, and it is called the science of management. The simple days of just the boss and the labor force are over: Between the two has come the "hierarchy," the "management structure," the "chain of command." There is little point in examining the reasons for this; they are too complex in detail, and too simple in essence. Once you accept that large organizations usually triumph over small ones, you accept that "managed" industries will succeed "bossed" ones. For the last hundred years, and with increasing rapidity in the last fifty, we have seen the small companies merging into larger groups: Today, most business organizations are far too large and complicated to be run by a single policy maker and decision maker. They have to be managed. Sometimes it seems that the old problems of making well and selling well become insignificant compared with the ghastly new problem of managing well. Management is the great new preoccupation of the Western world. General Motors has a greater revenue than any state in the union, and the fifty biggest corporations in the United States have greater revenues than the fifty states. The giant corporations have far bigger revenues than the governments of most countries. The wealth of nations depends increasingly on the quality of managers, and an ever growing number of the best people are managers, or intend to be managers, while all the rest find their lives directly and sharply affected by the decisions and actions of managers.

Almost more surprising than the rapid growth and spread of management is the apparent novelty of it. The study of the sciences has also developed with staggering speed in the last fifty years, but science has a long and distinguished ancestry, whereas management appears to have dropped out of nowhere. Peter Drucker, its high priest, says:

> The emergence of management as an essential, a distinct and a leading institution is a pivotal event in social history. Rarely, if ever, has a new basic institution, a new leading group, emerged as fast as has management since the turn of this century. Rarely in human history has a new institution proven indispen-

sable so quickly; and even less often has a new institution arrived with so little opposition, so little disturbance, so little controversy.

How can this have happened? How can the human race suddenly have adapted itself in millions to such a new basic institution? Only, I suggest, because management is not a new basic institution at all. On the contrary, it is an ancient art.

I can hardly think of a less auspicious way of starting a book on management than by disagreeing with a man who writes with as much knowledge and experience as Drucker. However, his remark quoted above is only by way of a preface to his book *The Practice of Management*, and no argument is built on it. Later on, in a similar aside, he says:

> There are hundreds, if not thousands, of books on the management of the various functions of a business: production and marketing, finance and engineering, purchasing, personnel, public relations and so forth. But what it is to manage a business, what it requires, what management is supposed to do and how it should be doing it, have so far been neglected. This oversight is no accident. It reflects the absence of any tenable economic theory of business enterprise.

Whether a tenable economic theory of business enterprise will ever be found, I do not know. And perhaps it does not matter; because I believe there is a tenable political theory of business enterprise. The new science of management is in fact only a continuation of the old art of government, and when you study management theory side by side with political theory, and management case histories side by side with political history, you realize that you are only studying two very similar branches of the same subject. Each illuminates the other, but since history has been studied to excess, and management hardly at all, it is not surprising that it is management situations that are illuminated more often.

It was Machiavelli who brought this truth home to me. Machiavelli is not at the moment required reading in business colleges or for management training courses. In his introduction to the Everyman edition, Herbert Butterfield, Regius Professor of Modern History at Cambridge, claims no modern relevance for Machiavelli's writings: "The chief significance of his work today," he says, "lies in the fact that it marks a stage in the development of the scientific method, whether in statecraft, or in general political analysis, or in the broader fields of history." And yet Machiavelli, however marginal his relevance to academic historians, is bursting with urgent advice and acute observations for top management of the great private and public corporations all over the world. You only have to know how to look for it.

Although the connection became clear to me in a sudden flash, a moment of what Arthur Koestler calls "bisociation," I can see that I had been working toward it for some time. I was one of the middle management of a large and growing corporation of some 20,000 people with a gross revenue around $100 million a year. I was fascinated, perhaps (in view of my lowly position) precociously fascinated, with the problems of management and leadership and organization, not just of that particular corporation but of any modern corporation that faces the problems of great size and continued growth. It seemed to me then that this scale of operation was still, for most industrial nations, such a new one that we were all probing, pioneering, and guessing, with few helpful precedents and little accumulated wisdom to guide us; each firm was working by trial and error, and all too often repeating the errors of others rather than learning from them.

I was discussing this at lunch with a friend who is chairman of an industrial engineering group. I asked if he and his fellow managers had formulated any laws or amassed a body of folk wisdom about the right way to treat a firm when you have taken it over. He had made some extremely interesting observations from his own experience: One of them was that a staff of four hundred represents the critical number in a firm taken over. It is the number that separates the personal boss from the high-level manager. You may run a firm of four hundred or fewer people extremely well, but that is the maximum you can run personally, knowing all their names, without too much delegated authority. If the firm is expanded to, say, 1,100, it may destroy the boss: Instead of knowing all people by name, they become pegs on a board; instead of just doing and deciding, you have to do a lot of explaining and educating; instead of checking up on everything yourself, you have to institute a system and establish procedures. All this demands skills quite different from those you built your success on, and ones you may well lack.

This, however, was only an isolated observation. There did not seem to be any generally accepted body of opinion, any guiding principles, for the taking over of firms, even though it was (and is) one of the chief problems facing thousands of top managements all over the Western world. Many managers had made their own observations, but they were not collated, and when takeovers happened every firm had to work out how to do it on its own, and from scratch.

The next day, while this conversation was very much in my mind, I was reading Machiavelli's *The Prince.* I thought I was browsing agreeably among the remote political problems of Renaissance Italian states, when suddenly I encountered a sentence that was so utterly relevant to the previous day's discussion that in a few seconds it transformed my attitude to the book, to Machiavelli, to management, and to political history. It seemed like a direct answer to the question of how you make a taken-over firm into a part of your own organization, capable of operating to the same standards and worthy to carry a part of your reputation. The passage (Chapter III) reads:

> The other and better course is to send colonies to one or two places, which may be as keys to that state, for it is necessary either to do this or else to keep there a great number of cavalry and infantry. A prince does not spend much on colonies, for with little or no expense he can send them out and keep them there, and he offends a minority only of the citizens from whom he takes lands and houses to give them to the new inhabitants; and those whom he offends, remaining poor and scattered, are never able to injure him; whilst the rest being uninjured are easily kept quiet, and at the same time are anxious not to err for fear it should happen to them as it has to those who have been despoiled. In conclusion, I say that these colonies are not costly, they are more faithful, they injure less, and the injured, as has been said, being poor and scattered, cannot hurt. Upon this, one has to remark that men ought either to be well treated or crushed, because they can avenge themselves of lighter injuries, of more serious ones they cannot; therefore the injury that is to be done to a man ought to be of such a kind that one does not stand in fear of revenge.

In other words: "Put small management teams of your own into one or two key factories, because otherwise you'll use up half your staff in giving orders and issuing requests, and then checking that they've been properly fulfilled. By comparison a management team does not cost much, and the only people who will be upset are the former managers whose jobs they have taken over. And since they are no longer in the firm, they cannot cause any trouble, while the rest of the staff will not protest as long as they still have their old jobs, particularly while they have the example of the fired managers to keep them on their toes. The guiding principle is that senior managers in taken-over firms should either be warmly welcomed and encouraged, or sacked; because if they are sacked they are powerless, whereas if they are simply downgraded they will remain united and resentful and determined to get their own back." This, though Machiavelli does not mention it in this context, is the principle on which the Romans founded their empire (which was one of the most spectacular examples of successful large-scale management); generosity (full Roman citizenship); or brutality (executions and enslavement, full military garrisons); but not the sort of half-hearted severity that left the defeated enemy resentful and still in being. Since reading that passage I have tried out Machiavelli's principle on several managers who have had to cope with takeovers; they all agree with him.

Of course this might simply have been a happy coincidence. Many writers have taken elegant analogies from history—the British Broadcasting Corporation has been most persuasively compared with the democratic centralism of the Soviet Union—to decorate or illuminate their observations on management. But this seemed altogether too close to be an accident; and the next chapter of *The Prince*, when looked at in this new light, also became extremely relevant and up-to-date:

> The principalities of which one has record are found to be governed in two different ways: either by a prince, with a body of servants, who assist him to govern the kingdom as ministers by his favour and permission; or by a prince and barons, who hold that dignity by antiquity of blood and not by grace of the

> prince. Such barons have states and their own subjects, who recognize them as lords and hold them in natural affection. The examples of these two governments in our Time are the Turk and the King of France. The entire monarchy of the Turk is governed by one lord, the others are his servants; and, dividing his kingdom into sanjaks, he sends there different administrators, and shifts and changes them as he chooses. But the King of France is placed in the midst of an ancient body of lords, acknowledged by their own subjects, and beloved by them; they have their own prerogatives, nor can the king take these away except at his peril.

Anyone who has worked in large organizations must instantly recognize these two basic methods of management. The British civil service is well known to be Turkish in outlook, rotating managers (especially at the lower levels) at a hectic speed. The Foreign Office is particularly religious in its observance, making sure that none of its embassy staffs stay for more than a few years in one place. This, according to Machiavelli, ensures that the goodwill and hopes of benefit of the foreign governments are directed toward the central government in London, and not to the person of its representative. It is the sort of organization that often develops under a very tough and strong top executive. According to Machiavelli, it is very hard to force or intrigue your way to the top of such an organization, but comparatively easy to run it once you are there.

At the other pole, the Frankish organization, it is much easier to take over the top position, but much harder to achieve anything when you reach it. When a strong and active leader is succeeded by a weak or lazy one, the organization will tend to revert from Turkish to Frankish— the barons are strong when the king is weak. Oxford and Cambridge universities are notorious examples of the Frankish system—it is entirely suitable that the body appointed to inquire into the running of Oxford University should have been known as the Franks Commission. The feudal baronies are the colleges, and the heads of colleges rule them from appointment until retirement with as much freedom from interference as they can arrange. And they arrange it very well; the central government of the university comes under the chancellor, a figurehead, and the vice-chancellor, who is the head of one of the colleges appointed for one year only in strict rotation—an excellent way to ensure that the power of the colleges is never reduced. It is the autonomy of the colleges and the impotence of the university that have always defeated university reform.

The BBC television service, when I belonged to it, was another excellent instance of Frankish government. All the programs of any consequence were produced by four great departments—drama, talks, light entertainment, and outside broadcasts. They were four powerful baronies, and the barons of the last three had all succeeded to the title after being heir apparent (assistant head). And they had been baron or heir apparent for ten, nine, and seventeen years respectively. The fourth was new, but his predecessor had been baron for nine years, and heir apparent for one year before that. In that time there had been all sorts of convulsions in the central government: First there was a controller with an assistant controller, then a second controller with no assistant, then a third controller with a new assistant, then the same controller with two chiefs of programs, and then shortly after I left a fourth controller with two chiefs of programs. It was the continuity of the barons that smoothed out these convulsions; but, according to Machiavelli, it must have meant that the new rulers found it difficult to exercise much control over the actual domains of the barons—the content and quality of the programs they produced.

A few pages later there is another parallel, of particular significance to the manufacturing industries. To translate it into modern terms, Machiavelli discusses whether you should, ideally, manufacture and assemble your product entirely in your own factory, or whether you should contract it out to associated companies, or to independent contractors. He argues that associated companies are liable to their own industrial disputes and production and delivery crises that are beyond your control and of a higher priority to them than your order; that independent contractors will delay or drop your work if a much more lucrative urgent contract crops up; that if you succeed with a product that another firm is making for you, then you place yourself at their mercy; and that you should therefore make everything you possibly can in your own shop. Few production managers would question this conclusion. In fact, he expresses it in terms of whether you should defend your state with an army formed by your own citizens, or with auxiliaries, or with mercenaries; he points out that allies may withdraw (or withhold) their troops if they are attacked themselves; or, if they fight and win, that they will then start dictating to you; that mercenaries are always liable to desert to another prince, or even to your enemy, if he pays better; and that an army of your own citizens is the only one you can really trust. The differences are differences of application; the principle, being rooted in human nature, is the same in both cases, and is just as valid now as it was 450 years ago.

The root of the matter is that the great modern corporations are so similar to independent or semi-independent states of the past that they are understood best in terms of political and constitutional history, with management most properly studied as a branch of government.

# 2

## THE STATE, THE CORPORATION, AND THE DEVIL

In all important ways, states and corporations are the same—in particular in the framework they construct within which economic and political necessity interact with the people's minds and wills. States and corporations can be defined in almost exactly the same way: institutions for the effective employment of resources and power through a government (board) to maintain or increase the wealth of the landowning classes (shareholders) and provide safety and prosperity for their citizens (employees). The competition of commercial and industrial rivals, strikes, the problem of getting the most advantageous trading situation with the least possible sacrifice of independence—all these problems are in their essence the same as enemy invasion, civil rebellion, or alliances with other states that have a common interest or a common enemy. Cartels and price rings are only a form of treaty, placing a limit on areas of conflict at a time when continued warfare is likely to damage all the combatants more than it can reward them. As one General Electric executive said at the time of the great electrical industry antitrust case of the 1950s: "Sure, collusion was illegal, but it wasn't *unethical*. It wasn't any more unethical than if the companies had a summit conference the way Russia and the West meet."[1]

Of course there are certain superficial differences: In particular, (1) corporations do not meet in military conflict, (2) they do not have absolute authority over a geographical area, and (3) a member of the staff of, say, General Motors does not belong to General Motors in the way a Russian belongs to Russia or an American to the United States. All these points are worth examining.

## Military Conflict

The first transference you have to make when studying political history in management terms is to read "economic conflict" for "military conflict." Corporations compete just as keenly as states, and are impelled by exactly the same human emotions of greed and fear and pride, or self-interest and opportunism and a desire for security, or whatever else you believe to be the root of human competitiveness. Corporations do not exist in a state of constant war any more than states do; it is when one of them tries to break into an export market previously dominated by a rival, or manufactures a new product cheaper or better than one already marketed by another, that you have a situation comparable to war and invasion. But a great deal of the conflict between corporations, especially as they get larger, is confined to frontier skirmishes or guerrilla warfare, where each side tacitly accepts its share of the market (its territorial limits) and is more concerned to safeguard what it has than to make any dramatic advances. Corporations, like states, can exhaust themselves by too much warfare, just as they can become fat and lazy from insufficient exercise. But this transference only points up the comparison: A sales director planning an assault on a rival's market needs exactly the same qualities as a general planning an invasion: not just courage and a steady nerve, but, more precisely, knowledge of the enemy's strength and weakness and how strong his reserves are and how fast he can mobilize them (e.g., has he the capital to step up his advertising, the capacity to step up his production, the margin to cut his price, the sales force free to intensify his selling); what the strength of his own force is and its endurance, how far he can push them, what ground they fight best on (which sort of product they sell best and which worst); where the likely counterattack will come (price cuts, advertising, etc.) and how to meet it—these sorts of comparisons can go on almost endlessly, since the essentials are identical and only the superficialities are different. The difference between killing and selling may, objectively, be rather more than superficial, but not in the qualities they demand of those planning and executing the campaign.

## Authority Over a Geographical Area

This difference is even more superficial than the previous one. It is only important if you try to compare corporations with present-day states: but it is not in modern Britain and Russia and the United States and France that the comparison between corporations and states lies. If it were, it would have been obvious long ago. Modern states incorporate a number of nineteenth-century concepts, like nationalism and universal suffrage, which (at least so far) are not embodied in the great corporations; but if you go back to prenineteenth-century states, the parallels become much clearer, and particularly if you look at the continent of Europe rather than Britain: Britain developed the idea of nationality (and nationalism) much earlier than most of Europe. A sixteenth-century Italian state, or a German city-state of the seventeenth century, is better understood as a tract of land owned by men or families than as the tight, highly organized, and highly governed nation-state of today. And just as modern corporations own their land, their offices and factories and refineries and oil wells, not absolutely, but under a higher authority, so many of those earlier states held their authority under the Pope or the Hapsburgs or the Bourbons; nevertheless it was, for practical purposes, theirs, just as Seattle is, for practical purposes, Boeing's and Wilmington is DuPont's. The interplay between groups of human beings and tracts of land, according to one of the greatest modern historians, Lewis Namier, is the essence of history. For most of history, tracts of land have been the only source of wealth. If by "tracts of land" you can now include factories and refineries as well as mines and oil wells and farmland, and if you can also include sales areas, home and overseas markets, then the essence of history can be distilled from the modern corporation just as it can from the earlier states.

## Belonging to the Country

This also depends on comparing corporations with pre-nineteenth-century states, before the state came to mean the same as the nation and the race, when much of the Polish nation was in Prussia, the Czech in Austria, the Greek in Turkey. If you were a wandering artisan traveling through Italy in the sixteenth century and spending a year or two in Naples and then in Florence and then in Venice, you would not feel you were in a new country or a new state in the modern sense; you would be much more like an American computer programmer, say, working for IBM for a couple of years, then for Apple Computer, then for Microsoft. You are always primarily an American citizen under the general authority of the United States government, though while you are in the different firms they profit from your labor and you take your salary and follow their staff regulations and policy rulings. In the same way, the Italian artisan was under the general authority of the laws of Christendom, and the individual laws of the separate states were much more like company regulations, and while there you would observe their laws and pay their taxes but not feel as much of either a citizen or an alien as a modern traveler in different countries. The citizens of those states were much closer to employees of the king (or prince or duke) than to citizens of a modern nation-state. It is not unreasonable to look on their citizenship in terms of a contract of service: They were employed by the king to create wealth for him (taxes) and when necessary give him security (military service) or help him enlarge his territory and dominion. In return he protected them (with an army they might serve in) from the depredations of enemy states, and guaranteed that they would not have their land taken away by the force or fraud of their fellow citizens (legal system). But they had few if any civil rights: If they incurred the king's displeasure then they could be jailed or executed with no trial and no appeal. Their consolation was that they were all full citizens of the kingdom of Christ, that before the throne of God their soul weighed as heavy as the king's and that servitude on earth was a small price to pay if it would buy a ticket to the kingdom of heaven.

It is at this point that the parallel becomes uncomfortably close. For most of the employees of big corporations, the power of the government to make them happy or miserable is very small: An increase in the interest rate may slightly affect the cost of a mortgage; over a long period the establishment of a health service, the abolition of military service, the building of roads, the preservation of the countryside, and so on may raise the general quality of their lives; but what the government does it does for everybody—they all rise or fall together. The power of the firm over their lives, however, is far greater. They can be told to go and live in another part of the country, or an other part of the world, or to desert their wives and children for months or years: they can be publicly exalted in the eyes of all their colleagues, the people whose respect they most prize, or publicly humiliated, passed over in favor of a subordinate; and these are not things that happen to all alike, but specifically and personally to them. Of course they are free to resign, just as the Neapolitan could go and live in Venice; but he might arrive with a record and a reputation, Venice might be no more congenial, and a person has to live somewhere. So the computer expert, the employee of a computer company, has not much alternative but to work for another computer company—and explain why he left the last one; and a person has to work somewhere too.

The government is like Christendom, an overriding system of law that only very marginally affects the actual physical conditions of people's lives, but gives them an illusion of equality in that their vote weighs as heavily in the ballot box as the chairman's or the managing director's. In the important part of their lives, their forty years of work, they have none of the freedoms that matter: No political freedom—the corporations rarely have the courage to risk the customer and community antagonisms that might be aroused by an executive who campaigned for a political party or ran for election on a party ticket; no freedom to publish—they cannot write newspaper or magazine articles without clearing them with the corporation, and according to *Industrial Marketing* "an important part of the company spirit is the forfeiture of the pride of authorship";

no freedom of speech—if they gave their subordinates or the press details on the incompetence of their board they would be liable to be fired, and if this is not the death penalty it can still shatter one's life as much as banishment; no right of trial, and no judiciary that is independent of the executive—their career can be blighted and promotion stopped for utterly unjust reasons such as the personal whim of a hostile nobleman (director); and they have no sort of representation in the councils that decide how the firm shall be run, no say in its government, however much the decisions may affect their lives. The twentieth-century junior manager in Standard Oil or Ford lives in a state of voteless dependence on the favor of the great, just like the sixteenth-century Italian.

A corporation, in fact, is not something different from a state with some interesting similarities: It is a state, with a few unimportant differences. A corporation has its king and its barons, its courtiers and ambassadors, its loyalists and its dissident elements, its allies and its enemies. What *is* important to our understanding is not the superficial differences but the underlying unity.

The most remarkable demonstration of this underlying unity is Book II of *Paradise Lost*. Nothing, you would think, could be further from the twentieth-century corporation than Milton's epic account of the fallen angels taking counsel about their expulsion from heaven: a biblical story recounted by a seventeenth-century poet. And yet as you listen to Satan and his crew discussing what action they can take, you realize that in every important respect the situation is that of a corporation trying to formulate a new policy after taking a terrific beating from its chief competitor and being driven out of the market it had previously depended on. The language is high poetry, but the arguments are, *mutatis mutandis*, exactly the arguments that would (or should) be considered in the boardroom of any corporation in a similar situation.

Satan makes some introductory remarks and then asks for proposals; there are four speakers; Moloch, Belial, Mammon, and Beelzebub. Moloch speaks first and says:

> My sentence is for open war: of wiles,
> More unexpert, I boast not.

and goes on to talk in emotional language about fighting back: he is the classic instance of the unintelligent, unimaginative, bull-at-a-gate executive with masses of drive and no brain; he is contemptuous of those who want to think and plan:

> ...let us rather choose,
> Armed with Hell's flames and fury, all at once
> O'er Heaven's high towers to force resistless way
> Turning our tortures into horrid arms
> Against the torturer...

In other words, "don't let's stop and analyze what went wrong or reconsider our general policy; let's just raise more capital, reequip the factories, boost our advertising, train more sales staff, and try again." Most firms have a Moloch, and he is usually an invaluable man so long as he is told exactly what to do. He uses energy and emotion as a substitute for thought, and instead of thrashing out policy, picks out the simplest solution because it is all he understands. He gives away the emotional basis of his arguments by his last line, admitting that he is advocating an aim.

> Which, if not victory, is yet revenge.

Belial is the exact opposite; highly intelligent, and although his critics would call him a pessimist or a defeatist, he would probably call himself a realist. He starts by neatly accomplishing the admittedly rather simple task of destroying Moloch's arguments,

> First, what revenge? The towers of Heaven are filled
> With armed watch, that renders all access
> Impregnable...

and then goes on to propose an alternative plan, which in fact is not a plan at all: It is to accept the inevitable:

> ...this is now
> Our doom; which if we can sustain and bear,
> Our supreme foe in time may much remit
> His anger...

In other words, "Let's accept our defeat, accept that we're a small firm now and not a big one. At least we still exist, and if we putter along, circumstances may one day change and we may have a chance to get back again, whereas if we take Moloch's advice and fail we will not exist at all." Belial is the exact opposite of Moloch, the brains without the nerve.

Mammon is the first to propose a viable and thought-out policy. But he starts by dismissing an idea not yet mooted, namely, asking to be taken over by the company that has licked them. Not for him the specious cant about "not being in the long-term interests of shareholders"; he goes straight to the heart of the matter, and voices the emotion that (whatever the circular may say) is uppermost in the breast of every director threatened with a takeover by a victorious rival: the humiliation of it.

> ...with what eyes could we
> Stand in his presence humble, and receive
> Strict laws imposed, to celebrate his throne
> With warbled hymns, and to his Godhead sing
> Forced hallelujahs; while he lordly sits
> Our envied sovereign?...

In recent years many taken-over directors and executives in defeated corporations have learned what it is to sing forced hallelujahs, and most of them would share Mammon's views about it.

Mammon also joins Belial in ridiculing Moloch's idea of war. He then goes on to propose an alternative to acceptance of the inevitable, namely, developing the possibilities of hell:

> ...This desert soil
> Wants not her hidden lustre, gems and gold:
> Nor want we skill or art, from whence to raise
> Magnificence; and what can Heaven show more?

and he urges them

> To found this nether empire, which might rise,
> By policy, and long process of time,
> In emulation opposite to Heaven.

Or, put another way, "Let's start developing the few products we have left, and perhaps develop some more along the same line, and drop the products that we've been beaten on. Then, if we put our backs into it, we can be a big firm again, in different lines."

Mammon obviously caught the feeling of the meeting:

> He scarce had finished, when such murmur filled
> The assembly, as when hollow rocks retain
> The sound of blustering winds...

which was hardly surprising since he was the first to offer a real policy. But Beelzebub was still to come, vice-chairman apparently:

> ...Beelzebub...than whom,
> Satan except, none higher sat...

and also in league with him, because he puts forward the chairman's policy as if it were his own, so as to preserve the chairman's apparent impartiality:

...Thus Beelzebub
Pleaded his devilish counsel, first devised
By Satan, and in part proposed...

Beelzebub proposes the fourth possibility: Not fighting back blindly, not accepting passively, not developing new products, but seeking out new markets:

...There is a place
(If ancient and prophetic fame in Heaven
Err not), another world, the happy seat
Of some new race called Man...

and he suggests a preliminary market survey,

Thither let us bend all our thoughts, to learn
What creatures there inhabit, of what mould
Our substance, how endued, and what their power,
And where their weakness, how attempted best,
By force or subtlety...

And so they finally decide to go into the export business, so to speak; and it is Satan himself, as an example to all chairmen, who flies out to investigate and report on the new market. The language of Milton may be more compressed and highly charged than the normal board minutes, but all the arguments are exactly those that would be advanced in such a market situation. The interplay between groups of gods and tracts of the firmament is the essence of theology.

# 3

---

## *THE MACHIAVELLI METHOD*

It is of course the increasing size of firms and corporations that makes it possible to study them in political
terms. A small family firm can only be compared with a
small feudal estate, and since both are entirely and personally run by the head of the family there is little revelation
in the comparison. It is only as the commercial and industrial enterprises become as great and as complex as they
are today that they begin to take on the apparatus of states
and need to be studied as political institutions.

Some firms reach great size through their own organic
growth, without any mergers or takeovers: Marshall Field's
and Marks and Spencer (Britain's largest retail chain) are
classic examples. But these are the minority; most big firms
today have grown by acquisition, with the extremely complex problem of integrating all the different units they have
absorbed, of digesting what they have swallowed. This, of
course, is the problem I started with, the discussion about
how to treat a taken-over firm, for which there were no
established precedents. And yet it is hardly possible to read
history without stumbling over precedents on every page.
For example, the best-known event in English history, the
Norman Conquest in 1066, was one of the most brilliant
and ruthless takeovers ever recorded. Not the Battle of
Hastings, which was just a battle, but the twenty years that
followed it. In that time William I removed all but two of
the major English landowners from their manors and

replaced them with his own Normans—usually waiting for the excuse provided by an act of disobedience or rebellion, just like the chief executive of a taking-over firm replacing every senior executive of the acquired firm with one of his own men the instant they question a decision. Most of the land that he did not keep in the family or the church went to just ten Normans—a very reasonable span of command. The Domesday Book was the most detailed inventory ever made of capital assets and the annual revenue to be expected from them—and William was ahead of most modern managers in having the whole inventory checked by a team of assessors independent of those who took it. His Normans had to agree to an annual production target before being given the land—taxes and mounted knights—and agree to serve on central committees—the royal courts and councils. He also imposed a central personnel policy—in 1086 he made all the principal sublandowners in the realm swear to obey him, even against their own feudal overlords. Wherever an existing institution worked satisfactorily, he left it unchanged; where there was resistance, he was utterly ruthless. Incidentally, he was the natural son of the Duke of Normandy and a tanner's daughter. No one before or since has more fully deserved the name of bastard. But most takeovers need a bastard if they are to be as complete and as successful as his.

In fact, the takeover problem, so far from being new, has been the major preoccupation of government for hundreds of years. To quote Professor Butterfield again: "The work of fusing the smaller units into a monarchy, and turning the monarchy into a 'state,' the inhabitants into a 'nation,' was the main function of the institution of kingship in Europe between the tenth and the eighteenth centuries." I suspect that many people in top management today will instantly recognize that sentence as a neat statement of their own problem. Many of our large companies and corporations have become monarchies by a succession of mergers and takeovers, but they know that they are not yet a state, and their employees are not yet a nation. Their problems are the same because the circumstances that brought about the situation were the same: The king wanted the small principality, perhaps to secure a frontier, perhaps for its agricultural wealth, as a managing director wants a small firm to consolidate a section of the market or augment the larger firm's plant and labor force. The small principality and the small firm often welcome this absorption as an alternative to annihilation by another, more powerful rival. But having acquired the principality, the king finds it defends the frontier badly, leaves half its taxes uncollected, is liable to revolution that may spread, and sends its quota of troops to the national army under-equipped, badly trained, and with low morale. The managing director may find that the taken-over firm makes an uncompetitive product, has hopeless labor relations, a chaotic accounting system, uneducated management, and a poor sales force. He has, however, eight centuries of experience to draw on. The wisdom of princes is at the disposal of managers.

So we come back to Machiavelli. It is a pity that his name has become synonymous with sinister and unscrupulous intrigue—"murderous Machiavelli." It is also unjust; his main purpose was simply to analyze what practices had brought political success in the past, and to deduce from them what principles ought to be followed for political success in the present. It was an honest attempt at scientific inquiry; not surprisingly many of the courses that he discovered had brought political success were not such as to bring moral acclaim as well. As Bacon says, "He set forth openly and sincerely what men are wont to do, and not what they ought to do." As a result he has been ridiculed as an advocate of wicked and immoral actions, whereas his message is only: "If political success is what you want, this seems to be the most effective way to achieve it." *The Prince* is a work of extreme realism intended to sort out some guiding principles, based on his own experience of government, his deductions from observing the government of others, and his analysis of history, for the benefit of Giuliano de' Medici when he should take over his new principality. It is a selection of case histories of government on a number of well-defined and important questions: "Concerning the way to govern cities or principalities which lived under their own laws before they were annexed," "Concerning cruelty and clemency, and whether it is better to be loved than feared," "Concerning the secretaries of princes," "Why the princes of Italy have lost their states," and so on. It does not build a coherent system of political philosophy; it is essentially empirical, pragmatic, and practical.

I have called this book *Management and Machiavelli* not because it is based on Machiavelli's arguments but because it is based on his method, the method of taking a current problem and then examining it in a practical way in the light of the experiences of others who have faced a similar problem in the past. The problems are those of the large corporations in the twentieth century; the experiences are drawn indiscriminately from corporations and states, but because the latter are so much more fully and more truthfully documented, political history has proved a richer source than management case history. And, like Machiavelli, I have found problems on which, for lack of any other source, my own experience has had to provide most of my evidence; in particular for the chapters on creativeness. But whatever the source, I have tried to keep the book empirical, pragmatic, and practical. It is not a search for instances of history repeating itself or a system of management philosophy, but is, like *The Prince,* an attempt to analyze current and relevant management problems in the light of experience, observation, and history. Above all it is about leadership; Machiavelli called his book *The Prince,* and not something like *The Art of Government,* because he saw success and failure for states as stemming directly from the qualities of the leader. Success and failure for corporations also stem directly from the qualities of their leaders: Management techniques are obviously essential, but what matters is leadership. The word "leadership" has fallen into disrepute of recent years, chiefly because of the old Victorian concept of leadership as something that any middle-class English boy could be taught in ten years at boarding school before being sent out to govern the lesser breeds. It was a quality that did not need any special knowledge or qualification and one that was opposed to originality and imagination and nonconformism. It is now becoming accepted that leadership is not necessarily hindered by a deep knowledge and lifelong experience of the area in which it is leading, even if the battle to establish imagination as a prerequisite of leadership is not yet won. But we are now in danger of overcompensation, of accepting the rival heresy that success in industry can be achieved not by leadership at all, but by management science, without an individual of courage and vision and experience at the head of the enterprise to tell the management scientists what to study and for what purpose.

The trouble is that too much writing on management has been concerned not to examine it but to attack or defend it; and not on the legitimate grounds of whether it has been successful or unsuccessful, but in a fruitless quest to establish that its ultimate purpose and effects are moral or, alternatively, immoral. The Marxists' determination to prove that large private industries operate against the public interest has not only discolored their own writings; it has also discolored those of the non-Marxists, who constantly seem to feel an obligation to prove that, on the contrary, well-managed companies invariably operate in perfect harmony with the personal morality of those who work for them and the general good of the community they belong to. The corollary must be that any firm that makes its employees lie or pollutes the air with black smoke and the rivers with industrial effluent is on the road to bankruptcy; alas, experience does not always bear this out.

The only helpful way to examine organizations and their management is as something neither moral nor immoral, but simply a phenomenon; not to look for proof that industry is honorable or dishonorable, but only for patterns of success and failure, growth and decay, strife and harmony, and for the forces that produce them. A great volume of this sort of study has been applied to the minutiae of management, and those who are concerned with accounting systems or sales incentive schemes or media selection have a considerable library of dispassionate scientific analysis and recommendation to guide them. But people concerned with the organization as a whole have little beyond their own experience, the advice and warnings of their friends, a number of published case histories, and a few disguised tracts.

Perhaps this is not surprising. The simple business of designing and making a product that does what you said it would, and delivering it to the person who ordered it, on the day you promised, for the price you agreed, and then collecting the money and recording the whole transaction somewhere where you can find it when you want—to do this on a large scale and stay in business requires quite a number of separate bits of efficiency. Leaders of expanding organizations have an urgent need for this sort of efficiency, and there are not enough men or women who possess it. But there is an alternative: highly efficient systems, which can be operated by managers of much less natural ability with some confidence of success and little fear of disaster. And since most of these systems and practices and techniques can be taught and explained and written down in pamphlets or books, there is now a great volume of writing on all these practical aspects of management. But leading the whole organization needs wisdom and flair and vision, and they are another matter; they cannot be reduced to a system and incorporated into a training manual. And yet, as corporations grow larger and larger, it becomes more and more important to understand how they work, what forces operate within them and upon them, what makes for health or sickness, success or failure. Perhaps we cannot draw up rules for all occasions, but by a judicious use of the Machiavelli method we can learn to recognize which situations and problems are common to large organizations, and see the different results that tend to be brought about by different courses of action. "Historical parallels can never be drawn without risk," says Professor Hugh Trevor-Roper, "but general lessons can be extracted even from societies distant in time as in place." There are far more lessons from history than there are management case studies. This book attempts to detach managers from their preoccupation with inventory management, discounted cash flow, and project evaluation and review techniques, and to link them with their true predecessors: the kings, princes, prime ministers, generals, barons, cardinals, and courtiers who have been trying to cope with the same problems for the past two or three hundred years.

# 4

## FROM BARONIES TO EMPIRES

Drawing general lessons from history is by no means the same as discovering historical parallels. The former is academically honorable, the latter is altogether too slick and seductive. Moreover, once you are launched on an attractive parallel it is tempting to continue it beyond the point at which the evidence gives out and the facts withdraw their support. Any suggestion that history may be repeating itself is therefore likely to bring reactions ranging from pursed lips to blown tops. Historians may indeed repeat themselves, but not history.

And yet when you look at the rise of the great modern industrial corporation, you cannot avoid a most remarkable similarity between the developments in industry over the past 100 to 150 years and the course of English political history over the past 900. In history, the basic political unit of Anglo-Norman times was the feudal overlord with his manor, his surrounding lands and their revenues, and his more or less dependent peasantry; in industry it was the small independent manufacturer with his factory or workshop and its product, and his more or less dependent workers. The feudal boss would work simply through his secretary and his bailiff, the industrial boss through his clerk and his foreman: Neither would willingly allow to those he thought of as his dependents any of the measures of independence they from time to time demanded. The industrialist would stamp as hard on talk about union hours and rates as the baron on talk about the superiority of the king's court. To be an English baron in the twelfth century or an English manufacturer in the early nineteenth century was to exercise independent, arbitrary, and unfettered power to a degree that is virtually impossible in modern England.

And yet, despite their power, each lived in a state of profound insecurity. The baron had many rivals, some with richer lands and more money, who could march on his manor with a greater force of armed peasants than he could field. As time passed a few of them, perhaps with special dispensations from the wealthy church with its lands and monasteries and rents, would become far too large for him to attempt to resist if they should choose to attack him. The manufacturer too had many rivals, and some with more capital or better patents or cheaper labor or fewer distribution problems than he had: and as time passed, a few of them, perhaps with lucrative contracts from central or local government with all its rates and taxes, would become so powerful that they could undercut his prices and run him out of business whenever they chose.

Already the parallel looks suspiciously neat, and ought therefore to be discontinued; but, regrettably, it goes further. Gradually the barons with their small private armies were absorbed into larger units: On some occasions they were simply conquered, on others they made a deal with the stronger baron while they still had a few options open, getting his protection against other stronger barons in return for supplying him with men when necessary. The result was a smaller number of larger private armies, which finally clashed in the Wars of the Roses. They lasted for thirty years, and by the end most of the smaller baronies had disappeared for good. "Where is Bohun? Where is

Mowbray? Where is Mortimer?" lamented Lord Chief Justice Crew in 1626, "Nay, what is more and most of all, where is Plantaganet? They are entombed in the urns and sepulchres of mortality." And, like the barons, the small manufacturers found themselves unable to maintain their precarious independence: They could not compete with the broader base and greater capital of the bigger firms.

Some went bankrupt, and were bought up by the bigger groups, some made deals and became absorbed into the ever-growing corporations. A modern Crew might ask: "Where are Hughes Aircraft and RCA? Initials such as GM and GE are the sepulcher of a thousand famous industrial names."

The result, in English history, was the great York-Lancaster merger, the marriage of the Lancastrian Henry VII to Elizabeth of York and the foundation of the Tudor dynasty. For all but eleven of the next 118 years, from the accession of Henry VII to the death of Elizabeth I, England had a monarch of strong personal authority who was a focus of the loyalty and admiration of most of the nation. Internal conflict and revolt were firmly suppressed and gradually died away, and from a firm and united home base England was able to resist her European rivals and start building a colonial empire overseas.

In industry, you can frequently find exactly the same process at work, and indeed it is still continuing. After the multiple mergers and takeovers, there often emerges a large and powerful firm led by a member of the ruling dynasty, the family whose firm triumphed. The Vanderbilts and Rockefellers and Carnegies are the Tudor monarchs in the realms of railways and oil and steel. And once they have created unity and exacted or deserved loyalty from the small baronies that compose their new empire, they too fight off their rivals in their own field and start to turn their eyes to profitable and unexploited markets over-seas. Some of them even have the classic York-Lancaster merger—as, for example, the British computer industry. Employees of the two deadly rivals in the data processing business, Hollerith and Powers-Samas, came into work one morning to discover that they were all part of the same firm, International Computers and Tabulators. I think that if I had been its first chairman, I should have studied the early years of Henry VII's reign very carefully indeed. What is more, shortly after their Bosworth came their Armada: Spain, in the shape of IBM, launched the computer System/360. ICT too had been building a fleet, the 1900 series of computers: they knew they could not conquer IBM, as Elizabeth knew she could not conquer Spain, but they had to fight hard to prove they could survive.

(In passing it is interesting to reflect on the defecatory habits of the hippopotamus. The male indicates to other hippopotamuses the extent of his own territory by defecating all around its perimeter. Outside that ring they can go where they please, but if they come inside it he will fight them to the death. So, too, nations make a ring around their territory: To Elizabeth I, the wars in Holland were beyond the ring, but the Armada came inside it. No doubt the United States government wishes it had left Vietnam on the outside of its defecatory ring. And so, too, industrial corporations, consciously or unwittingly, make the same sort of ring around products and sales territories and sections of the market.)

The period of successful dynastic monarchy is often looked back upon as the golden age in history and industry, but it does not last forever. The dynasty cannot continue to produce great rulers indefinitely, and the increasing size and complexity of government and management make it harder and harder for an average or less-than-average ruler to get away with it. Moreover, this increase in size and complexity demands money on a new scale, and neither the king nor the dynastic industrialist can go on financing it from his personal fortune forever. The king depends more and more on the taxes he raises from his subjects; the industrialist, on the capital he can raise on the market. Consequently the king becomes more and more dependent on the good will of the merchants and financiers and landed gentry, and the industrialist on the approval of his bankers and shareholders. In history, all is reasonably well while those supplying the money trust the behavior and approve the objectives of the sovereign, but when you get a king like Charles I, oppressive in policy, unsound in finance, and delegating his authority to over-bearing or incompetent minister-managers, there is likely to be trouble. Characteristically, it was one of his taxes (ship money) that brought his assorted enemies together in con-certed opposition.

The execution of Charles I may be the most dramatic moment in the changeover from personal to parliamentary government, but the process started long before and ended long after: It is the progressive attenuation of the autocratic power and personal authority of the sovereign continuing from the thirteenth century to the nineteenth. In industry, the same conflict still goes on: Howard Hughes, it seems, was the Charles I of TWA, similarly forced into a corner by shortage of finance, and Parliament, the ten-year voting trust set up by the major stockholding insurance compa-nies to control his activities. The reason that Charles I could not have continued as king on Cromwell's terms is astonishingly well expressed in the explanation of why Hughes could not remain as head of TWA:

What made this impossible, put simply, was a fundamentally different attitude towards the company between Hughes and TWA's modern managers. The latter regarded the airline as an institution which, aside from the fact that it operated a vital national service, had an existence which should be independent of its ownership. What amazed and distressed them more than anything else was the concept of ownership as an expression of the proprietor's personal needs and circumstances.[1]

Hughes' difference with his managers about the relationship between the owner and the company, in fact, was almost precisely the same as the difference between Charles I and Parliament about the relationship between the king and the state. However, Charles got his head cut off and Hughes sold his TWA stock for $546.5 million; so there are certain differences.

TWA is only one case typical of thousands: The conflict between owner-bosses and professional managers, with bankers and insurance companies and other block shareholders weighting the scales on the side of corporate efficiency against capricious authority. In states and corporations, the end is the same: The powers of government pass away from the dynasty to the professional meritocrats, to the politicians and top civil servants; the powers in industry pass away from the family to the professional managers. In politics it is called "the century of the common man," in industry "the managerial revolution."

Obviously there are points in this analogy where details do not coincide exactly, but there is a clear pattern for the development of successful enterprises, whether political or industrial: First the small rival baronies (or states or city-states or tribes or firms), then the emergence of a few larger ones and perhaps the absorption of most of the remaining small ones by the great leader-figures, and last the transition to the corporate state. All these stages are visible at the moment in different nations and different industries: In America, computer software is emerging from the small-barony stage, with a few bigger units pressuring many smaller firms. Publishing and electronic communications are in the process of unification, with the corporate giants becoming established; and the automobile and aerospace industries are well into the corporate stage. In politics, too, it is still happening; and the political development of African and South American states causes pain to their liberal well-wishers in the West as they obstinately persist in going through the stage of strong, personal autocratic rule on their way from tribal society to the corporate state.

# 5

## THE KING AND THE BARONS

The struggle between the king and the barons is the great recurrent theme in the domestic politics of medieval England. Sometimes the barons are up and the king is down (Stephen, John, Edward II); sometimes it is the king who is on top and the barons who are repressed or quiescent (Henry I, Henry II, Edward I). There was a time when I found it puzzling that England should have bouts of tearing itself to pieces in domestic strife, even when there were great dangers threatening (or great opportunities beckoning) from outside her borders. After all, they were all part of the same kingdom, weren't they? Surely they could see the advantages of all pitching in together? Now, after working with a number of large corporations, I find the behavior of the rulers of medieval England just as unwise but far less surprising. Few employees of any large corporation are so naive as to say, "After all, we're all part of the same company, aren't we? Why can't we all work together to beat our competitors instead of wasting our time on all these internal wrangles?" Most are far too well aware of the strength of the internal rivalries and jealousies. I know of a case where one great company missed a marvelous opportunity to enlarge its share of the market by such a factor that it would have become the leader instead of the runner-up in its field. Their chief competitor ran into grave cash-flow troubles that they themselves, for special reasons, escaped. But they did nothing. It was not that they did not see the opening; they saw it, and they took action. But the actions were little more than gestures, and the reason was that their real energies were absorbed by a full-blown baronial war. One of the senior managers, with the known sympathy of some members of the board and an important corporate shareholder, was trying to get control of two other departments and some important production resources. Other managers were resisting bitterly. Long, passionate memos were being placed before some executives and passed behind the backs of others. The talk in dining rooms and bars was of nothing except this all-absorbing internal conflict. Managers spent the journeys to work and back pondering nothing except the next move in the battle; they talked about it endlessly to their wives, and lay awake half the night thinking about it. Resignations were mooted and threatened, and preliminary secret approaches made to other companies. In short, all the thought and energy and passion that should have gone into the sales and promotion drive were diverted into the baronial war. When it was over, the opportunity had passed.

The reason, of course, was the same as in medieval history: When the king is strong the barons are weak; when the king is weak the barons are strong. And strong barons fight and plot to become stronger, at the expense of the king or other barons or both. In this case, strong leadership would have stopped the war before it started; the reorganization would have taken place at once or never; and the only criterion would have been the good of the company, not the relative strengths of feeling of various people within it. Instead, the king was playing politics. Kings should be free to play foreign politics; they should not have to play domestic politics.

There is a constant danger of baronial war in any large organization, and it is the first and surest sign of weakness at the top. The first duty of government, according to political and legal theorists, is to preserve order within the realm; the first duty of management is to prevent baronial warfare. Politically, we have learned to suppress riot and civil strife, but industrially we have not. Frank Pace, who took over General Dynamics from its founder, Jay Hopkins, in 1957, found himself virtually a prisoner of his own feudal barons. His total head office staff numbered 200, in a company of 106,000 made up of nine divisions that were all virtually corporations in their own right. Most of them had been independent enterprises before they joined, and had their own separate legal and financial staffs and, of course, their tough baronial presidents. Pace decided to leave them more or less alone. "The only way to succeed," he said, "is to operate on a decentralized basis." If William I had thought that, the Battle of Hastings would now be regarded as an unimportant raid instead of a turning point in history. As a result of its feudal, baronial structure, General Dynamics managed to lose $425 million between 1960 and 1962, the biggest product loss ever sustained by any company anywhere.

Britain's (aptly named) power industry provides another spectacular case of strong warring baronies. The three great nationalized boards charged with running coal, gas, and electricity were in constant and vicious competition with each other—and not just in advertising and selling and lobbying against each other, either: Householders on new estates were offered electricity installation at cut rates on the condition that they not install gas as well. It would have taken a powerful king to discipline three such barons; instead, their activities were "coordinated" by the Department of Energy, which was also responsible for

North Sea oil and natural gas. Anyone who expected a smooth and integrated fuel policy for the UK under such a setup must have been totally ignorant of baronial emotions and practices, but connoisseurs of baronial warfare watched the battles with reprehensible delight.

Contact with large organizations also provides a useful corrective to the stereotype of the wicked, power-mad baron. I suppose there are people in management who seek power for the sheer pleasure of exercising it, but I have never encountered them. Most people who aspire to power within organizations will tell you that they want it so as to achieve objects they believe in, but even that does not go to the heart of the matter. The real pleasure of power is the pleasure of freedom, and it goes right back to one of the most primitive human needs, the need to control the environment. You get no great sense of freedom if you are liable at any time to starve or freeze or be devoured by wolves or speared by a neighboring tribe, and so you set about securing a supply of food, shelter, warmth, and defensive weapons. Gradually you increase the control, and one of the most important ways you increase it is by organization, by making your tribe the biggest and strongest in the area, and of course by doing so you submit yourself to the control of environment again—the environment now being the organization you belong to—a much more agreeable one than before, but still outside your control. However, if you become a respected and successful person within the organization, you may begin to be involved in the control of it. You taste what some people call power, but to you it tastes of freedom. Your life is still partly regulated by the actions and decisions of others, but now a part of it is regulated according to your own choice and by your own decisions. You are regaining control of your new environment. Finally, you become head of a whole division—

production division, say. Only the chief executive stands between you and the sky; only his budget allocations, his overriding decisions, his general policy rulings, his overall plans, his vetoes, keep you from total control over your environment. He may see them as curbs on your power, but you see them as barriers to your freedom.

Suppose he is a new chief executive. At once you want to know how far he will restrict your freedom in practice. You have an important project that will cost more than the $250,000 you are allowed to authorize, but only a little more. You know it is unlikely to be authorized for this year if you put it up. So you cost it at $245,000 and "discover" later that it cost $275,000. What you are doing, in hippopotamus terms, is defecating on territory he has enclosed within his defecatory ring. (There is a colloquial term for this that is very similar in its drift). Only just over the edge, but over it. His reaction will soon tell you if you can try it again. If he is a weak king, you will quickly gauge that you can go further, and soon you will discover all the apparatus of baronial infringement of royal sovereignty at which the English medieval barons became so expert. They withheld tithes, you overspend your budget. They barred the king's officers from their castles, you withhold information and returns. They failed to contribute troops to the king's army, you cannot spare any staff to go and help start up the new subsidiary in Buenos Aires. They substituted feudal justice for royal justice, you pursue an independent personnel policy. And every time you get away with it, you take a little control of your environment away from him and appropriate it for yourself.

The trouble is, of course, that you are not the only one playing this game. The research and development manager is playing it, too. So is the sales and marketing manager. And now it is not the weak king but the other strong barons who are the obstacles to your freedom. The stage is set for a first-class baronial war.

Suppose you are the king, and not a baron. What do you do about this situation? The obvious answer is that you do not let it arise, but the sad fact is that from time to time it does. After all, it is not only a problem of top management; it can happen with equal intensity, if diminishing significance, right down the management line. And if it is pointless to give advice to the executive who has let it happen, there is still his successor to be considered. What do you do if you inherit a corporation or division or department that is in a state of baronial war?

There are of course the conventional exhortations: Make it clear from the very start exactly where you stand, show them at once that you don't stand for any insubordination, etc., etc. The trouble is that you are likely to be to some extent on trial yourself, and if the barons who are divided in everything else are united on the fact that you are a menace, you are not likely to last long enough to reap the fruits of your firmness. There are, however, a number of techniques that have been employed by strong kings when succeeding weak ones, and they are all worth consideration.

To start with, it is essential to realize that you have a baronial problem, and that you are unlikely to achieve any real external success until you have quelled the internal strife. And then it is a great help if the baronial wars have been going on a long time. In the early stages each baron is anxious to try out his strength, and some may be strong enough to think they could emerge as top baron and become king. Some even do, which creates quite a different situation. But if you come in fresh to a war that has been going on a long time with no final victor, and especially when there is danger from overseas in the shape of competitors' products and sales drives, then there is likely to be a general wish for some sort of order and stability imposed from above.

Such timing cannot always be arranged. But it usually seems a good idea to direct attention firmly to real or potential threats from overseas, or to necessary offensive action to forestall them, so that internal conflict can be made to appear a sort of treachery. ("Look, if we can't get production up by 20 percent we won't be in business at all next year. So for God's sake let's solve that one first and argue about who authorizes the staff increase later.") It is unwise to provoke any general issue of the king's power, as a question of principle, in the early stages. Much better to make an alliance with one baron and pick off the others singly for pragmatic, practical reasons. ("It's simply that if I don't get your capital expenditure forecast in more detail and earlier, it makes nonsense of the planning committee meeting.") The kings used to go out periodically and knock down the barons' castles; withheld information and un-referred decisions are the bricks that corporation barons build their castles with.

Another useful device is to take over, for a time, direct control of the least efficient barony. This is difficult and demanding for a king who has the whole realm to run, but Churchill combined the Ministry of Defense with the office of prime minister during the war. It may be risky for the king to go into battle himself, but if he fights bravely, and wins, it can secure his position like nothing else. If the chief executive takes over production for six months, straightens it out and gets it flowing smoothly, all the other corporation barons will suddenly fear that he might do the same to their divisions. Their strongest weapon, the threat of resignation, suddenly falls to pieces in their hands.

Some kings have also built up a royalist party. It is a dangerous game, because once it becomes apparent, the king is seen to be playing domestic politics, bidding for personal loyalties in return for personal favors. The ultimate aim of the corporation king is to command the complete trust, respect, and loyalty of the whole board and management; and a royalist party is a great obstacle.

For many kings, the answer has been to turn to the great capitalists and enlist their aid against the barons. King and capitalist are natural allies; the king wants a kingdom at peace, and a kingdom at peace gives a better return on capital than a kingdom divided by civil strife and baronial faction. In the corporation kingdom, the large block-voting shareholders are the capitalists. If they support the managing director when he wants to sack the director of production, his hand is greatly strengthened for dealing with the other barons. The danger, in kingdom and corporation, is that the king may fall too much into their power; that he may merely exchange the military defiance of the barons for the financial compulsions of the capitalists. Nevertheless, most kings would probably think it a fair exchange.

The most powerful weapon in the war against the corporation barons, however, has usually turned out to be money. The sovereignty of Parliament over the crown was established when Parliament controlled the king's revenue, and the practical head of the government was for many years known simply as First Lord of the Treasury. So long as the corporation king retains that control, he is well armed. The corporation barons always want money— more money than they can have. The king will give it to them according to the overall needs of the corporation, but if he is clever he can tie it up with a wider plan that somehow involves the knocking of a few more bricks out of their castle wall—the supplying of more information, or the referring of more decisions. The money, after all, is their means of controlling their environment, of putting their plans into effect, running their division the way they want to. If it means trading in a less significant instrument of environment control, the deal is worth doing.

None of these devices can be applied to every situation, but I suspect that there are few successful chief executives who have not used them from time to time, even if they were unaware of their stately pedigree. The final aim is to get into a position where the barons can be moved, promoted, or rotated at the wish of the king without any internal strife. This does not mean that he actually will move them; indeed, so long as they know that he can, they are likely to take pains to ensure that he does not have to.

# 6

## THE AMERICAN PAPACY

What should be the relationship between government and industry in the modern world? This is a very fashionable question, and brings in so many considerations, such as industrial freedom, national security, fiscal policy, state control, national planning, and the like, that there is hardly an editorial writer in the country who cannot fall back on it in times of news shortage. But at the root there is only one question, and it is a question of power, practical power: How far can the government control industry and get away with it? And this leads on to the question of what the instruments of a government's power are and how it employs them; not the theoretical, legal instruments embodied in the statute books, but the practical ones for everyday dealings.

To understand this, you must compare a modern Western democratic government—say the government of the United States—with the medieval or Renaissance papacy. Not the modern papacy: Despite its not inconsiderable influence on national and international affairs, it is by no means the force it was in medieval Europe. In the Middle Ages it was the center and focus of a geographical area known as Christendom; and the idea of Christianity was more than a personal faith, it was the moral standard of Christendom and a political rallying point against the great and menacing enemy who embodied the opposing idea of Islam. In just the same way, the United States president does more than embody the philosophical concept of democracy and a free society: He has been the trustee of the political standards of the West, and the rallying point against threatening powers who embodied the opposing idea of communism. To renounce Christianity for Islam in the Middle Ages was not to make a private decision about your own worship, it was to threaten the security of all Christians, who were busy keeping (or failing to keep) the armed forces of Islam out of their fields and towns. You might have no thoughts of treachery, but you would have a job to prove it, just as American communists have had a job proving they are loyal to the state they belong to despite subscribing to the opposing political theory. Korea and Vietnam are the First and Second Crusades, with Mao Tse Tung or Stalin as the Saladin of the twentieth century. There are historians who believe that rising productivity in eleventh-century Europe, with the consequent population growth, caused grave land shortage, which threatened to lead to civil disorder, and that Pope Urban II's preaching of the First Crusade helped to siphon off the surplus population, especially younger sons, with the hope of conquests and new lands in the East. There are commentators who believe that fear of slump or recession prompted the United States government into expanding its armament program for economic reasons, and that the prolongation of the war in Vietnam was aided by the panic on Wall Street every time there were rumors of peace.

It may be that in theory even the medieval pope was not supposed to exercise direct political power over the states of Christendom; the dispute as to whether ultimate authority rested with the pope or the emperor was as prolonged and inconclusive as the argument about government and industry today. But in practice his power was considerable. To start with, there were the papal states, which made him a political ruler in his own right, with men and armies at his command—armies that tough prelates, and even a strong pope like Julius II, might lead into battle themselves. It also gave him the patronage of political and military offices within the papal states as rewards or incentives to men he wanted in his service. Then there was the church within the states of Christendom, the faithful with their spiritual and hence, he could argue, political loyalty to him. It is true that the bishops were often appointed not by him but by monarchs or corporations in the various countries, and that they might prove stupid or difficult from time to time, but they were still his people. Then he had his own cardinals and legates at the court of every country. Then there were the religious houses dotted about all over the place, and each reporting back to the head of its order in Rome. There was the canon law and the papal courts to enforce it. And above all there were the papal revenues, collected from all over Christendom; these could be used to put an army in the field, or to dangle in front of the kings and princes as an incentive to take the action he wanted—Pope Sixtus V pledged Philip of Spain a million gold ducats at the time of the Armada, to be paid when the first Spanish soldier set foot on English soil. The result of all this was that whatever the result of the doctrinal argument between pope and emperor, a decisive pope with a full treasury was a powerful political force.

Now we come to the American pope, the president of the United States, and his dealings with the corporations. He certainly has his papal states: the Administration, the armed forces, NASA, the Department of State—all these make him a major employer, and a major industrial customer, in his own right. Like the pope he has the patronage of many powerful and desirable offices of state to attract or reward the people who serve him. And the presence of this patronage moderates the behavior even of those who do not seek it, since there are few who can be sure that they will never seek it. He also has the local governments, the state legislatures with their officers and mayors and state governors. Like the bishops, they are not appointed by him, but elected locally; nevertheless, bishops often had attractive ideas that needed papal authority or papal cash for their execution, and the state legislatures are often suitors to the federal government in the same way. The pope could use the bishop's pressure on the king to conform with his policy as part of a deal, and the United States government can act in the same way. It is by no means impossible that Ford might want permission to expand onto state-owned land outside Los Angeles, and the consent of the governor of California would be vital. The government of California might be applying for a federal grant for a new university, or lobbying for a new army training center to be built in California and not Nevada. And the government might want Ford to keep a slightly uneconomic plant open in a depressed area because of the jobs it provided. And so, although the local government posts are not in the federal gift, they can still be used in the federal cause. This practice is sometimes called wheeling and dealing; I prefer the old term, "diplomacy."

As well as the state legislature, the government has its equivalent of legates and cardinals; these are the government officials and inspectors supervising the government contracts within the firms and the federal officials of the area. Has it also its monastic orders? One of the great advantages of the orders, from the pope's point of view, was as an information network. They had their own valuable local functions, of course—as hospitals, for instance—but they were not subject to the local church; they reported back direct to Rome. Because they were so closely integrated with the community, they got wind of all information very quickly and sent it back regularly, so that events even in remote lands rarely came as a surprise to the Vatican. It would be perfectly easy for the president to have monasteries; for instance, teams of U.S. Air Force personnel permanently based at the main Boeing, Lockheed, and General Dynamics factories and working with the development and production staff on design details and modifications from the user's point of view. They would use the Boeing canteen, the Boeing recreation facilities, but they would report straight back to the head of their order in the Pentagon. And so any snags on the contract, or substandard equipment, or large unbudgeted cost savings, or use of government contract people or time or plant for commercial jobs, would get back to Washington at once. I wonder if the president has monasteries?

The president also has his canon law as distinct from civil law. The McCarthy inquisition for the rooting out of heretics is an example that springs naturally to mind, but the United States antitrust laws, too, are nearer to canon law than civil law. To violate them is to offend against the god of Competitiveness, which is an important part of American industrial-religious faith of which the president is trustee and guardian.

But of course the greatest single source of papal power was the Vatican treasury. The president collects his revenues from taxes rather than tithes and annates, but they give him similar powers. Where the pope could offer a million gold ducats to Philip, the president can offer huge government contracts to IBM and AT&T and Texas Instruments and General Motors and Lockheed and Boeing—all the great states of Christendom. No wonder they fall over themselves to anticipate his wishes; for instance, by making sure that plenty of their subcontractors are in politically important depressed areas when preparing their bids for new contracts. Few popes can ever have been as strong as the American one. It is not just the profit from doing the work that attracts them; it is the research and development the work entails, that pay off in commercial products for years to come. Because of this, the wishes of the government in other matters can have the force of commands. If Exxon raises its prices at a time when it might damage the overall economy, it is told to lower them again; and it does. When General Motors announces a cutback in production at a time when Wall Street needs confidence in the continuing boom, it reverses the announcement within twenty-four hours because the president tells it to. Its humble obedience is only exceeded by the Emperor Henry IV standing barefoot and clad in sack cloth in the snow outside Canossa on a not entirely dissimilar occasion. In fact, this same power can be used to discipline states that have superficially more independence from the United States government than the United States industrial firms: It was the threat of withdrawn financial support that forced the government of the United Kingdom to break off the Suez action, and demonstrated that papal consent was necessary for any future military action. Modern Islam is not the enemy of the pope of Washington, D.C.—although individual Islamic states or leaders may be.

The modern pope-emperor argument still continues in Britain: to nationalize or not to nationalize? A glance across the Atlantic ought to make it clear that a modern government can leave this sort of discussion to the academic schools. As long as the government contrives to collect its taxes and places large contracts with industry, it has all the control it wants as long as it chooses to use it.

Compared with the medieval or Renaissance papacy, the American papacy looks fairly secure. The most likely danger is that of one state becoming too strong. The pope was weak when one state was so much more powerful than the others, because he had no choice but to look to that state for military support, and the king (e.g., Charles V) could more or less hold him to ransom. In the same way a government that must have computers is in a weak position if there is only one firm in the country that can supply the ones it needs: The firm knows the American pope has no alternative, and is therefore not submissive to his wishes. In addition, it is able to charge as much as it likes. And so the president has an interest in having a number of good and powerful firms in every field instead of a single dominant one, as the pope had an interest in there being a number of strong states. But the president is much better able, by the judicious placing of contracts, to restore the balance of power, and it was not at all surprising at the time of IBM's dominance to learn of the U.S. Air Force order for 150 computers from Univac. The modern state, therefore, has not only got control over industry by consent, it also has a vested interest in breaking monopolies in a much more beneficial and sensible and practical way than the cumbersome procedure of the law courts. While the political theorists go on arguing, the problem has solved itself behind their backs.

# 7

## RENAISSANCE AND REFORMATION

Historians have noted a pattern that frequently recurs in the rise or revival of states: first a renaissance, a period of military or political or commercial success, bringing about quick and fairly extreme internal social change, with new groups suddenly becoming much richer or poorer, much stronger or weaker, relative to others; then a reformation, a radical change in ideas produced by the intellectual turmoil that accompanies the political turmoil; and then—sometimes—a counterreformation, in which a somewhat reconstructed old order reasserts its former authority.

This same sequence of renaissance, reformation, and counterreformation also happens inside corporations. The renaissance occurs when one department or division or region suddenly has great success, and success that is obviously going to continue and grow. It might be the initially small computer section of a big airline, the new and expanding petrochemical division of an oil company, the group working on interactive television in a big electronics firm. Whatever the cause, the result is usually the same—increase in budget, increase in lab space, quick promotion for young employees, salaries worked up to invidiously high levels, recruitment of top-class people from inside and outside the firm, and an air of confidence that those outside the group prefer to call arrogance.

Then what? Then, you approach the stage known as "critical mass." Technically this is a term used in nuclear physics to describe the concentration of atoms of uranium 235 which causes an explosion: When you get a certain number in a certain space the mass explodes spontaneously. But in certain circumstances, there can also be a "critical mass" of people. Comedians are well aware that with too small an audience it is not possible to get a real laugh, and moreover that it is not absolute numbers but concentration that governs this: Two hundred people dotted around the Radio City Music Hall are not enough for a burst of laughter, but the same two hundred crammed into a small club are plenty. It is also probable that there is a relationship between critical mass and strikes. They tend to occur at points where there is the greatest concentration of people working, not necessarily in unions with the largest membership: Workers on docks and mines and in great car factories frequently strike, whereas farm laborers and shop workers, though forming a huge total number, are widely dispersed in very small groups, very rarely strike, and yet are among the lowest-paid groups in the working community. The railwaymen gave in before the miners in 1926, and railwaymen are the more dispersed of the two: Fewer vast mass-hysteria meetings, less group pressure on the doubter and dissenter, harder in fact to get the critical mass you can achieve at the blow of a whistle on the docks or in the mines. In 1848 a revolution occurred in Europe wherever there was a town with more than 100,000 inhabitants.[1] Equally, when Louis XVI summoned the States General (for the first time in 175 years) in 1789, he brought together the critical mass that precipitated the French Revolution.

So, in a growth area of a corporation, there is always a possibility of critical mass of managers, research scientists, skilled artisans, and other key employees. Not every mass is automatically critical; there seem to be two essential ingredients; a sense of grievance and a sense of power. A labor force may have a strong sense of grievance, but they would be foolish to strike when there is a lot of unemployment or when the firm is losing orders and about to cut back: They need a sense of their power to damage the management by striking before it becomes worthwhile. In the same way an expanding and successful department is not likely to go critical until its members know their value to the corporation, and know that the corporation knows it too.

When they reach that stage, a sense of grievance is fairly easy to come by. They may just feel underpaid, or undervalued, or underpromoted, compared with people doing less valuable and responsible work in other parts of the corporation, or they may feel the firm is making wrong decisions or is badly organized or incompetently managed. They talk about these things to each other at great length and with deep feeling; and if there are enough of them working in or around the same area, they begin to approach a critical mass and the stage is set for a reformation.

The essence of a reformation is that it is a power bid harnessed to an idea, and the idea usually involves reform of the whole institution of which the reformation group is a part. But the idea, the intellectual element of a reformation, is not the cause of it, and defeating the idea with intellectual arguments will not quell the revolution. It is the power bid that comes first; intellectual rationalizations follow. If the Russian peasants are shouting that the land belongs to the people, it is no good demonstrating by sound demographic, ethnological, and philosophical arguments that in fact it does not. Luther's theses, if nailed to the church door four hundred years earlier or four hundred years later than they were, would not have produced the same convulsions in Europe. The engine might be the same, but at those other times there was no steam to drive it. Similarly, if the expanding robotics department of a large machine tool company claims that representation on the board is too heavily weighted in favor of old conventional machine tools, it is no good demonstrating to them that this is not so. It may indeed not be so, but attempting to prove it will not still the movement that provoked the claim. It is like a doctor treating the symptom without diagnosing the disease.

A reformation movement can, of course, take any number of different forms, from mild unrest to a mass walkout. It is perhaps worth looking at the extreme case, as the Reformation in England and Germany were extreme cases. It could happen to a branch of a national trade union working in a far more prosperous and successful sector of the industry than most of the rest of their members. The employers might want to make a deal with the union which would be blocked at the national level because of its implications in other sectors of the union; but the local union is anxious to make the deal as it means trading in a few unnecessary safeguards and restrictions for considerable additional wages. If they then formed themselves into a separate union and proceeded to negotiate independently, it would be close to what happened where extreme reformers got hold of the church in the early sixteenth century. Or take the case of the great oil companies: How long can they stave off reformation in the great oil fields of South America and the Middle East? As they train more and more nationals to run the oil fields, they are hastening the day when a critical mass of, say, Kuwaiti managers realize that they can run the oil field on their own and that they would have much more power and freedom and wealth if their masters were the Kuwaiti government and not some distant board in Amsterdam or London or New Jersey. If that sense of power is allied to a sense of grievance, a reformation would certainly be in the cards. And the grievance need not be over pay or promotion: Clemenceau once forecast that the British Empire in India would founder not on the rocks of political injustice, but of social insult.

The classic error, which produces reformations, is for the management, whether pope or board, to give too little and take too much. If the church leaders of a country realize that they are doing all the work and contributing a great deal of money to the Vatican, while getting nothing in return except restrictions, vetoes, unwelcome commands, and a stream of indulgence peddlers who bring them all into disrepute, then they are ready for an idea like *Cujus regio, ejus religio,* which is a declaration of independence masquerading as a general proposition. If the local managers of an oil field realize that they are doing all the hard work, making all the difficult decisions, contributing huge profits, and getting nothing back except requests for information, directives, rulings, and a string of arrogant European or American executives who give the whole company a bad name, then they are in a reformation situation too. It only needs an inspiring leader with a general proposition, such as that the oil in a country belongs to that country (*Cujus regio, ejus oleum*), to start a worldwide movement; and the spectacle of the wealth of the oil-marketing companies and the poverty of the oil-bearing countries would influence public opinion much as the spectacle of the luxury and extravagance of the Vatican influenced it in the sixteenth century. As with the Reformation itself, the greater the geographical separation, the more likely the reformation becomes. The historic OPEC oil price increases of the 1970s attest to the reformation accompanying the growth of the oil-producing countries' power.

The process of giving too little and asking too much has had its most obvious demonstration in the dispute between Britain and Rhodesia. For forty years Britain had contributed very little to the solution of Rhodesia's internal problems, and Rhodesia had built its own political and industrial organization, which was strong and self-sufficient. Suddenly, when she saw the way things were going, Britain jumped in and tried to exercise her central authority, like a father who has not taken the slightest interest in his grown-up daughter's life until suddenly she starts staying out for the night, and then he begins laying down the law. So she just leaves home—there is nothing to stay for that makes it worthwhile to sacrifice her independence and submit to the central authority, and she is capable of supporting herself economically. Rhodesia was not receiving enough from Britain to make it worthwhile submitting to her authority: It was a simple balancing of profit and loss and the profit of Britain's friendship was outweighed by the loss of Rhodesia's freedom to choose the government she wanted. It is immaterial, in these terms, that Britain may have been right. The fact is that over the years she had let herself dwindle, in the eyes of those running Rhodesia, from the mother country into an agreeable irrelevancy. When she became disagreeable, Rhodesia exposed her irrelevancy.

How do you cope with a reformation? You can of course clamp down with extreme severity, but this is unlikely to be successful and may do great and lasting damage. After all, the revolutionaries, the reformers, are likely to be among the most valuable people in the company, and their leader, if he is capable of leading the most radical-thinking group in the most successful department of the company, is not likely to submit quietly to reactionary repression, and yet would be a serious loss to the company if he were to leave, as well as an invaluable acquisition for a competitor. Six such people, by leaving one company and joining another, altered the whole balance of power in the United States computer industry. Luther was not only a powerful and successful reformer, he was a tragic loss to the Catholic Church. Satan had been an exceptionally promising angel.

Fortunately it is characteristic of reformers to try to work their reforms peacefully within the framework of their organization. Only when that becomes impossible do they seek to overthrow it from within, or desert it for a rival; Walter Chrysler tried to get his proposals accepted by Durant of General Motors before he finally stormed out to found his own corporation. Many reformations could perhaps have been caught at an early stage, before they started to rouse violent feelings within the group and equally violent opposing feelings outside it. But if a counter-reformation is to be mounted, the key lies in the fact that successful counterreformations grow from the same soil as the reformation they counter. If, therefore, a corporation suffers from a Luther, it should start looking for a Loyola. Loyola's inspiration sprang from the same source as Luther's: dislike of luxury, criticism not of the faith but of some of its bad practitioners and mistaken teaching, concern for ordinary people, vigorous intellectual discipline, and extreme austerity of life. Loyola, indeed, was denounced (unsuccessfully) to the Inquisition for his unorthodoxy—evidence of how the successful counterreformer is likely to arouse as much suspicion among the establishment reactionaries as the reformer himself. Indeed the chief difference between them lies in the way they are treated by their superiors; Macaulay, in a famous passage, states that the church of Rome thoroughly understands what no other church has ever understood—how to deal with enthusiasts—and asserts that at Oxford Loyola would have led a formidable secession, whereas Joanna Southcott at Rome would have founded an order of barefooted Carmelites. (Even so, the church of Rome slipped up over Luther).

All corporations have their enthusiasts, indeed they depend on them, and it is for those in authority to choose whether to try to repress them and make them Luthers who will lead their enemies, or to encourage them to stay as Loyolas, to use diplomacy, courage, and imagination to give them a task, a responsibility, a mission, that challenges their intellectual skills and satisfies their emotional needs to the full, while still keeping them within the fold. Loyola was given the founding and leading of a new monastic order, the Jesuits. The corporation Loyola may be satisfied with the starting up and leading of a new product division or subsidiary company or research and development team; and even if he does not do it as successfully as he believed he would, it may still be better for the corporation to risk containing a failed Loyola, so as to insure against being opposed by a successful Luther. It may still be better for Standard Oil to appoint an Arab or Latin American president than to become the marketing organization for the great government oil companies of Iraq, Iran, and Venezuela.

# 8

## *CENTRALIZATION OR DECENTRALIZATION?*

To centralize or not to centralize? The discussion is never resolved, but the balance of emphasis is constantly shifting on the fulcrum of truth. At present, decentralization is the fashionable idea; no doubt it will be superseded by centralization in a few years' time, when the evils of misguided or excessive decentralization begin to make themselves felt. But the illusion that one or the other is the right way to run a corporation is likely to persist.

In favor of the decentralizers, it can certainly be said that excessive centralization is a common error that can do extreme damage to an organization. Most people are familiar with the pattern: the ever-lengthening delays while the head office makes up its mind, the futile attempts to lay down universal laws and procedures however inappropriate to the special circumstances of those affected, the top people growing more and more out of touch with the day-to-day realities, the individuals who work close to the products or customers having to refer decisions that they have the knowledge and experience to take correctly up to people who have neither, the stillbirth of enterprising ideas because of the frustration of waiting for the go-ahead until it's too late, or getting it in time but hedged in with reservations and modifications that make success almost impossible. But, of course, the dangers of excessive decentralization are just as damaging: production schedules being drawn up without consulting a sales forecast, two representatives—one from the region and one from the product division—trying to sell the same product to the same customer while providing conflicting facts about it, sales drives aimed at a volume of orders that the factories cannot in fact meet, good young managers bottled up in inadequate jobs because their bosses will not release them for promotion in other departments and have no vacancies in their own, and the general state of affairs where the planning department is an expensive joke and the firm has as many policies as managers.

Obviously, neither of these situations is desirable; equally obviously, a compromise that combines elements of both is not particularly desirable either. The trouble is that so often the argument between centralization and decentralization is the argument between two different kinds of bad management—the former nearly destroyed Ford, the latter nearly destroyed General Motors—and although they are both bad, they are mutually exclusive— they cannot coexist in one firm. But that is not to say that good centralization and good decentralization cannot coexist, or that a corporation cannot have a great deal of both.

The nature of good decentralization can be seen most clearly in the way states used to establish colonies. Athens and Rome in antiquity, Venice and Genoa in the late Middle Ages, Spain and England after the Renaissance, as well as many other great empires, achieved greatness by colonization. There are other ways—conquest, for instance, when your nation defeats a weaker one, and its king submits to your rule and agrees to an annual tribute. That corresponds to a simple kind of takeover, where you do very little with the taken-over firm except appropriate its profit. Colonization is different; it is the opening up of virgin territory, or land that is sparsely populated and almost completely undeveloped. The founding country says to the colonists, in effect, "Off you go. Here's a map, and this is where you'll be founding your colony. From now on it's up to you. We don't really know what the potentialities of the place are, any more than you do, but from the reports of travelers they certainly look reasonable. Whether you stay as a little fishing community or build a great city as splendid as ours really depends on yourselves. You may even come running home in three months.

"Of course we'll help you if we can: If you need supplies or armed reinforcements, we'll send them if we have them to spare. But don't depend on us. The idea is that we shouldn't interfere at all, and that you should become rich enough to send money back to your families at home, and contribute a good chunk to the upkeep of our army and our fleet, for all our sakes. And at least there's more future for you in going than in staying here."

When a corporation alerts a small production and marketing group to a completely new product, or sends a small sales team out to a region or country where they have never tried to sell before—in any new situation where promotion prospects can be limitless, depending entirely on the success the team makes of the enterprise—this is colonization. It is by no means the same as running a department within a company or a division, and the difference is in the degree of freedom. The best example I have encountered of the opposite of a colony was my own position when I was head of a program production department in the BBC Television Service: If I wanted to take on a new production assistant or pay an incumbent one more money, I had to apply to the establishment department; if I wanted to promote someone to producer, I had to apply to the appointments department; if I wanted a film editor to work on Saturday, I had to ask the film department; if I wanted to change a set designer, I had to ask the design department; if I wanted new carpets or an extra office, I had to ask the administration department; if I wanted to change studio rehearsal times, I had to apply to engineering allocations; if I wanted to tell the press about a program, I had to do it through the publicity officer. There was no question of doing without an extra office so as to pay a producer more—all these budgets were unconnected, and none controlled by me. And none of the heads of these departments worked under the head of my own group, and many did not meet a common boss until three or four levels up in the hierarchy; three of them only met in the post of director-general. The opposite situation would be the owner of a small independent production company; he would have total control of the gross revenue, and total discretion as to how he applied it; he would take on and lay off freelance designers, producers, and film crews entirely according to the needs of the program he was producing, and telephone the newspaper he chose whenever he had anything to talk about. Obviously, the difference in degree of freedom between those two situations is very considerable, and the closer someone is to the second, the more truly can he be said to be building a colony; and unless he has quite a lot of these freedoms he cannot be said to be in a colony at all.

There are several reasons why it is advantageous for the corporation to put managers in charge of colonial groups. If you know that your salary, success, self-esteem, and status in the corporation are limited only by the limits to which you can raise your colony, you are likely to put more into it than if they are limited by your boss, company career policy, and the grading structure. Also, this sort of independence has a powerful liberating effect on latent or suppressed creative and leadership qualities. It may not always be possible to give this sort of independence, since many jobs are too closely integrated with others, but a reorganization can often create more jobs that are colonial in type at the expense of others that are more like departments of the civil service. One of the most important reasons for colonization is a by-product of the conventional management hierarchy; it was also one of the most important reasons for the founding of colonies by the states of the past; not the pull from without, but the push from within.

It is obvious that if a corporation needs to go into a new line or a new market it will need to form a colony. That is the pull from without. But it may be just as important for it to colonize for internal reasons, because of the push from within, and that is likely to be less obvious. But very often the cities and states started colonies because there was no scope, no land, for the young men within their own boundaries. Rome and Athens were surrounded with hills, and beyond there were other states or cities that made expansion impossible: the only way to make a fortune was to pack up, get on board ship, and sail off to a colony. The Norman invasion of England and the First Crusade thirty years later have both been ascribed to this push from within Europe because of increasing population and restless younger sons wanting wider opportunities than their homeland could supply. It was this urge to get away rather than the pull of a remote El Dorado that supplied the motive force for colonization, and acted as a safety valve to prevent mounting tension and internal strife.

The conventional management hierarchy is rather like an enclosed city-state: A young manager can look around and see the mountains that circumscribe ambition. If you draw the diagram of the organization, you see at once that the higher you go, the fewer jobs there are; at every level, more and more people are squeezed out. Not necessarily forced to leave, but forced to reconcile themselves to not progressing beyond the level they have reached, or only one level beyond it. Each year the bright young people from the universities flock in far greater numbers than there are top jobs that will need their abilities. A static hierarchical firm will watch some of them leave at the time when they are about to be of most value, and see others fail to grow to the stature of similar bright individuals re-cruited by the firm in the days of its youth. People grow to the stature to which they are stretched when they are young, and the ones who are not stretched will fail to grow; some will actually be diminished. Corporation executives may tell you that an organization cannot have too many good managers, but they are wrong. What it cannot do is keep them good without constantly giving them tasks that match up to their abilities. This is why a firm may need to initiate projects for which there is no clear external reason, in order to make sure that staff of high quality stays with the firm—and stays of high quality.

So much for the nature of "good" decentralization, the foundation of colonies; it is close to the principle some-times called federal decentralization, but its nature and advantages are better emphasized by thinking in terms of colonies than of the United States. There is, however, noth-ing inherent in colonizing that prevents the ill effects of bad decentralization, the fragmentation and conflicting objec-tives and practices referred to earlier. For this, good decen-tralization needs to be accompanied by good centralization; and so far from being in indirect proportion to each other, they are in direct proportion—the more you have of the latter, the more you can afford of the former.

It is arguable (though I have no intention of arguing it here) that one reason why the Roman Empire grew so large and survived so long—a prodigious feat of management—

is that there was no railway, automobile, airplane, radio, paper, or telephone. Above all, no telephone. And therefore you could not maintain any illusion of direct control over a general or a provincial governor, you could not feel at the back of your mind that you could ring him up, or he could ring you, if a situation cropped up that was too much for him, or that you could fly over and sort things out if they started to get into a mess. You appointed him, you watched his chariot and baggage train disappear over the hill in a cloud of dust, or his trireme recede over the horizon, and that was that. If there was a disaster you would know nothing about it until months later when a messenger came panting up from the port of Ostia or galloping in down the Via Appennina to tell you that an army had been lost or a province overrun. There was, therefore, no question of appointing a man who was not fully trained, or not quite up to the job; you knew that everything depended on his being the best man for the job before he set off. And so you took great care in selecting him; but more than that, you made sure that he knew all about Rome and Roman government and the Roman army before he went out. To become a general demanded a long apprenticeship in a highly trained and very well-organized army. To become a governor, a man had to be a proconsul, a former consul, in other words he had to have held the highest office of state, before he was entrusted with the government of a province. This ensured that he never needed policy guidance or rulings when he was on the spot, since in any case there was no means of his getting them. It had to be there, deeply ingrained in him, before he set out.

Of course, you cannot run an empire without any communications—it will not be an empire, only a group of small, isolated states seeing occasional explorers. The

Romans had an excellent communication system—command of the sea routes (a large part of the empire was maritime) and a superb network of roads. They could therefore move armies, send reinforcements, supply garrisons, and do all that was necessary to protect their frontiers, keep internal order, and hold the empire together. But they were never under the illusion that they could pick up the telephone and save the sum of things for the price of a long-distance call.

In general, the long-distance telephone is a magnificent instrument for transmitting and receiving information and advice and suggestions, but an appalling one for exercising control. As a disgruntled British admiral growled after the Suez operation, "Nelson would never have won a single victory if there'd been a telex." The good sort of centralization is where the provincial governor or regional manager is "centralized" within before assuming a decentralized post. St. Augustine once gave as the only rule for Christian conduct: "Love God and do what you like." The implication is, of course, that if you truly love God, then you will only want to do things that are acceptable to Him. Equally, Jesuit priests are not constantly being rung up, or sent memos, by the head office of the society. The long, intensive training over many years in Rome is a guarantee that wherever they go afterward, and however long it may be before they even see another Jesuit, they will be able to do their work in accordance with the standards of the society. They may constantly face new situations and unfamiliar problems, but they will handle them exactly as the head of the society would himself, because they are so efficiently centralized internally. Perhaps this concept was most neatly expressed by Reay Geddes, the head of Dunlop, when he was telling the head of their German organization how to lay out his new factory: "The trouble with you, Mr. Geddes," complained the German executive, "is that you will not let your subordinates have a mind of their own." "Mind, yes," replied Geddes, "will, no."

One of the great modern centralization/decentralization dilemmas was faced by Shell Oil, and it is said to have paid McKinsey's half a million dollars to straighten it out for them. It is hard to see how the problem could have arisen at all, but for the telephone and the airplane. In essence, it was whether geographical regions (South America, Far East, etc.) should form the provinces of the Shell empire, or functional divisions (production, marketing, tankers, etc.). Obviously Rome would perforce have made the geographical unit the province, but while Shell was spending its half-million dollars with McKinsey's it might have invested a further dime in a phone call to the War Office. The British Army has exactly the same problem with its field commanders and its supporting arms—Artillery, Signals, Engineers, etc. Like the Romans and the Jesuits, the British Army takes great pains to make sure that field commanders are really deeply ingrained with the thinking of the army as a whole: tours of duty abroad, spells at home, staff college, all to ensure that when they take decisions on their own, they take the right ones, or at least the best the army knows. The Signals and Artillery people are more specialized, and so at every level they are a rank below the field commander, and "under command." The Signals officer at the War Office may replace his chief signals officer, but while he is "under command" he has to obey the man who is internally the most centralized, who is as it were trained, selected, and trusted by Rome to govern the province. Shell has in fact come to a similar conclusion, and it is the local manager who is in charge. A top executive has formulated the new setup in a way very similar to St. Augustine's: "Each local manager has a great deal of delegation, but he knows, by God, that he is a member of the group."

There is one further argument for delegation, that is, decentralization, of the right type, and in particular for starting colonies with considerable independence. It is that one day this small, experimental unit may turn out to be the great growth point of the corporation, and may even be its salvation. The decentralized, completely self-contained limits of Christianity, the monasteries, were created by St. Benedict on this principle: that if everything in Christendom were destroyed except for one monastery, Christianity could still survive in that single cell, and it was in the monasteries of Ireland at the darkest hour of the Dark Ages that European learning and the Christian faith were preserved from the rising tide of Mohammedan and Viking conquest. The Roman Empire survived the fall of Rome because Constantine had already moved the center of the empire to the colony of Byzantium, like a punched card company that got into computers just in time to survive the crash of mechanical data processing equipment. But it had been Diocletian who started it, by taking the government of the empire around with him, wherever in the empire he happened to be visiting or fighting. He had seen, nearly 1,700 years ago, the answer to the problem of the huge, overgrown, overstaffed, extravagant, inefficient corporation steadily losing its share of the market: Move all the vital decision-making people and functions to another place, and let the old one cave in. If there is a promising, strong, self-contained subsidiary company to move to, the essentials can survive the disaster.

# 9

## *THE FEARFUL SYMMETRY*

They may not put it down on paper, they may not even mention it in discussion, but a great many administrators and managers carry in their heads a pattern of the "ideal" organization. That pattern is the classic hierarchy, the family tree; one person at the top, with three below him, each of whom has three below him, and so on with fearful symmetry unto the seventh generation, by which stage there is a row of 729 junior managers and an urgent need for a very large triangular piece of paper.

This mental picture is probably less clear about the exact function of the managers at each level, but it generally carries the assumption that each is supervising the work of those below him, passing down policy guidance from above, and passing up requests and queries from below, ensuring that those below carry out their duties and that those above have the right information for their decisions and that responsibility is carefully graded so that at each promotion a manager takes a little more of it, until finally one of the original 729 contemporaries gets to the very top and takes it all.

There are irrefutable advantages to this kind of organization. Discipline is usually good, errors in routine procedures rarely go unchecked, and if the very top manager is an exceedingly able executive he can usually make the whole organization jump to his command very quickly. It usually takes a long time to build, and it is at its most successful when the function of the organization is to control a very large number of people all doing more or less the same thing. It is the way most armies are organized—platoon, company, battalion, brigade, division, corps, army—and if you want to make a million men advance or retreat at a few hours' notice it is hard to think of a better system. I suspect that it is service with the army in two world wars that has imprinted this organizational pattern on so many managerial minds within the modern corporations, even though making a million men advance or retreat at a few hours' notice is a problem they can encounter very infrequently.

A good hierarchy should be very nearly foolproof. It takes time to build, of course, but in its building the responsibilities of each job are firmly laid down, the procedures are worked out and established; and when it has to move, all move as one. But it has grave disadvantages, and although they may not be sufficient to invalidate it as a way of controlling armies they make it highly unsuitable and even dangerous for almost all other modern, large-scale operations.

The first is its depressing effect on the human spirit. Every manager knows that whenever a vacancy occurs above him, the odds are 2 to 1 against his being appointed to fill it, and that even if he does get the job he is still carrying out someone else's orders. Only at the very top will he have the freedom to make the important decisions and formulate the plans according to his own judgment. And when he first becomes a manager the chances of his getting to the top are 728 to 1 against. The effect is like a large number of cars going down a broad track that gets narrower and narrower. The farther you get, the more have to pull off the road, until only one finally arrives. In human terms, a manager strives for promotion and reward and success up to a certain point, but, earlier or later, almost all realize that whatever they do they are not going to get much further. Some will leave; a great many of the rest reach a turning point, when they say to themselves, "The difference between going on bursting my guts and taking it easy is about $1,000 a year before tax. So I'm not going to try." They then change from aiming at the maximum possible to the minimum excusable; their ingenuity and energy are converted from the task of getting more power and money to that of giving less time and effort. They try to pass the rest of their time with the corporation in a spiritual recess.

Obviously, no organization wants to force the majority of its staff into this state; and yet there is an even worse danger in the hierarchical system, namely, that it grows rigid. It cannot reach any great size without success, quite considerable success, at some stage in its past history; but the hierarchical system enshrines and sanctifies the qualities that brought that success in the past, and continues to search for and promote managers with those qualities even when circumstances have changed and different qualities are needed. A hierarchical corporation that won its success and grew to its great size in the years when efficient low-cost production was the key to all markets is likely to appoint production people to its most senior posts. And such is the power of the ego that individuals tend to assume that others of their own kind are, in the end, the best sort of people, and when other vital appointments have to be made, the board, consisting of former production managers, is likely to appoint more production managers. The problems may have changed to marketing problems, but it takes considerable humility to realize that you are not competent to tackle the biggest problems, and only little ingenuity to convince yourself that the problems are still, at root, production problems. And you and the board chat about the great days thirty years ago when you reorganized and expanded six factories in a year and hit the jackpot, and you just know that, in the end, it is production people who will solve this problem too.

It may well be that somewhere in the firm are the people with the skill and knowledge and ideas to solve the problem. But the hierarchy has been reinforcing its own prejudices for so long that it cannot believe it. To quote Professor Trevor-Roper:

> Any society, so long as it is, or feels itself to be, a working society, tends to invest in itself: a military society tends to become more military, a bureaucratic society more bureaucratic, a commercial society more commercial, as the status and profits of war or office or commerce are enhanced by success, and institutions are framed to forward it. Therefore, when such a society is hit by a general crisis, it finds itself partly paralysed by the structural weight of increased social investment. The dominant military or official or commercial classes cannot easily change their orientation: and their social dominance, and the institutions through which it is exercised, prevent other classes from securing power or changing policy.[1]

A hierarchical corporation puts a great social investment into the qualities that brought it success in the past. Not only its management selection, but all its training and indoctrination are geared for what used to work. Postwar Britain was an excellent example of this sort of rigidity: Her great imperial successes fostered a belief that there was a certain kind of man who could do virtually anything, namely, the sort of man who in the past had been successful in building and administering empires—courageous, disciplined, reserved, honest, conformist, incorruptible, ascetic, a natural leader. Hundreds of schools were founded in the nineteenth century to produce such men, a whole literature was created to glorify them, examinations and selection procedures were instituted to make sure that the best of these reached the highest posts in the land. Not just in the services and the Colonial Office, but also the civil service, industry, banking, stockbroking, and nearly all the "commanding heights." Consequently, when the change came, shifting the emphasis to imagination, inventiveness, quickwittedness, toughmindedness, brashness, scientific brilliance, technical expertness, individualism, sociability, and other such alien qualities, the rigid self-reinforcing society of the British governing classes could neither succeed nor believe that such qualities could bring success. "The talent that once went into governing Britain now goes more and more into clothes design," wrote Anthony Lewis in the *New York Times* in 1966. The trouble was that governing Britain was not a *carrière ouverte aux talents,* and the real new export successes—in the pop record business and clothes design, for instance—were being won by the sort of people who were quite unsuitable for admission into the elite. They started up in new areas because they were excluded from the old ones. There is an old saying that Frederick the Great (1712-1786) lost the battle of Jena (1806); meaning that for twenty years after his death the army had perpetuated his successful organization instead of adapting to meet the change in the art of war. Perhaps it is Cecil Rhodes and Rudyard Kipling who were really to blame for Britain's decline.

If Britain is rather a large-scale, not to say biased, example, take the Singer Sewing Machine Corporation. After decades of prosperity and success and international renown, it started to go into a terrible decline in the 1950s. Donald Kircher, the new president who had the job of lifting them out of it, described it in words that could equally have been used of the Aztecs, the Incas, Darius's Persia, fourth-century Sparta, Manchu China, or Spain after Philip II: "Its very success led to the assumption that all the answers were found, and that all one had to do was do what one's predecessors had done before. Everything became ingrained. There were no outside influences acting on the Company. It became withdrawn into itself."[2]

At the root, it is the same cause: the shared assumptions of a self-perpetuating elite, and the consequent inability to cope with the unfamiliar demands of a radically changed situation. Ordinary changes are no problem, as long as they can be countered with the weapons the soldiers possess, the maneuvers they are trained in, and the strategy the generals have learned. It is when the change is so profound that all these are thrown into the melting pot—machine tools, production processes, marketing policy—that the big and hierarchical firm is likely to be the last to change.

Fortunately, the family-tree hierarchy is not the only possible structure for great corporations; there is another. But although it too can be drawn on paper, it is not just a way of reorganizing the mechanism; it requires a completely different attitude. I remember once talking to a successful theatrical director about producing a play. I assumed that he studied it extremely carefully and thought about it until he had a complete picture in his mind of how it ought to appear to the audience, then cast it and rehearsed it until the actors finally came as close as he could get them to the ideal production that was taking place in his mind. Not at all, he said. Certainly he read it and thought about it, but he only formed a broad general idea of what the play should be like. It was in rehearsal that it really started to grow, as the actors and he together discovered more and more meanings and nuances and possibilities. My method would restrain the play within the limits of the director's imagination; his liberated all the creative abilities of the cast.

My attitude was the attitude of the hierarchical boss: One person decides what shall be done, and all the others work under him to achieve it. His was the opposite attitude, and in management terms it is usually expressed as a cell structure; it is the principle behind good centralization. The change in attitude lies in the effort to get rid of restraints and checks and routine supervision and graduated responsibility, instead of the effort to create them. Instead of assuming that there is only one person in the corporation who is capable of taking complete and unsupervised responsibility for an organization, you assume there are several. Instead of creating jobs so that every manager is responsible to someone above him for everything he does, you create jobs so that as many managers as possible have complete freedom to run their own cells as they choose, within general guidelines of policy and budget laid down by the central cell, and so that they can rise in salary and stature according to how big, how profitable they can make their cell, rather than waiting for promotion to the next layer up. It is the organizational pattern laid down by St. Dominic when he founded the Dominican order: the self-contained monastery under the abbot, and the headquarters of the order at Rome, not an elaborate hierarchical system of divisional and regional and area managers each held more responsible as he gets more remote from the place where things are happening.

The engineering industry is full of examples of the wrong way to grow large. It started with a number of small cells, a boss with a few men in a shed, with a lathe and a milling machine and a drill. But when it expanded, it expanded the functions instead of multiplying the cells: It kept the same central organization, and tried to control fifty milling machines and seventy lathes and a hundred drills, in the same way it controlled one of each. That is why the whole batch production business is constantly bedeviled by inefficiency, error, and communications breakdowns. It is most interesting that the latest organizational theory in the engineering factory is to revert to the shed principle: to abandon the vast milling shops and turning shops, and create cells that are equipped to produce a complete part under one person's supervision. These cells have just a few of each machine tool, and the cells, or groups, are classified by size of job, precision, and batch size: small, nonprecision, large batch; medium, precision, small batch; and so on, each operated by a team of a dozen or fifteen men under a group leader, who is responsible for a single job from start to finish.

You can see the same error in other industries. Publishing, for instance. A publishing house may start with a small cell-group and then expand functions until it has a large editorial department, a large production department, and a large sales department—with confusion, misunderstanding, and irritation growing up in the cracks. These functional departments can get further subdivided into design, press advertising, copyediting, illustrated books, etc., with nobody except the chief executive ever seeing a single book right through—and, of course, he's too busy. Or it can expand in a cellular way—educational books, fiction, history, and biography, with a team and a team leader in charge of each, using all the central services of the company, but responsible for the total business in that area from buying or commissioning manuscripts, through editing, production, and publicity, right up to selling to retailers. The terms of reference of a cellular growth are determined by the market: the educational market, for instance, in which the members of the cell get ever greater expertness. The terms of reference of a hierarchical growth are determined by the internal convenience of the organization. If, after a time, the education division expands, it too can expand hierarchically along organizational lines (education-editorial, education-production, education-sales) or by cell multiplication along natural market divisions (science under 12, English and history over 12, etc.). The difference is that the head of education-production is only responsible for a process ("not my fault, should never have been commissioned, and anyway they gave it all the wrong sort of publicity..."), whereas the head of science-under-12 is responsible for a total product.

The great barrier to setting up cell structures is a misunderstanding of the problems of delegation. The picture of overburdened A who refuses to let his underemployed subordinate B do any of his work or take any of his decisions is the stereotype, but it is the stereotype of an unusual and unimportant kind of failure. The true corporation stereotype involves A, B, and C. Poor old B is perfectly willing to delegate to C, but he is terrified that A will jump on him if C slips up: consequently he makes C refer all the decisions to him, double-checks all C's work, thereby irritating C and ulcerating himself. Delegation can only happen if A assures B that certain categories and levels of decision must be left to C, and if they are taken the wrong way the corporation will hold C and not B responsible. In other words, it must be understood throughout the corporation that the leaders of cells are permitted, indeed required, to make many types of decision on their own responsibility, within the terms of the policy guidelines and budget allocations given to them. Without that clear understanding, no amount of organization diagrams can turn a hierarchy into a cell structure.

Of course, there are disadvantages to the cell system: The head of the firm does not have the quick and immediate control of the entire day-to-day operation; his influence is over the longer-term decisions only. It would not do for an army in the field. But the cell system has four considerable advantages.

1. *It eliminates levels of command.* Efficiency, after all, is measured at the extremities. You do not find the efficiency of an army at general headquarters, nor of a firm in the head office. It is at the remotest point—the private soldier or humble legionary on the distant frontier, the woman at the information desk or the branch-office junior sales representative—that the really decisive test of an army or a firm is made. It is there that all the instruction and knowledge of relevant facts and procedural disciplines bear fruit—or wither on the tree. A hierarchy has been described by Thomas Burns, Professor of Sociology at Edinburgh, as a system where information goes up through a series of filters, and commands and prohibitions come down through a series of loudspeakers. In the cell system these layers are removed; each cell reports direct to the central cell. Some cells are large, some are small. No one pretends that the head of a small cell is equal in status or salary to the head of a large one; but in a cell structure you abolish the presumption that all those who report to the same person are equals, and consequently you abolish the need to make the head of a small unit report to someone irrelevant, for reasons of status jealousy rather than operational need. You can even draw some cells the size of dimes and some the size of quarters if it makes people happier, so long as all the lines go straight into the central cell. The chief executive may normally deal with the cells through a group of senior executives, but they are part of his central

cell and dealing as deputies for him, not a separate layer on their own. Together with him they form the command group, the cabinet, which governs the whole corporation. The heads of cells are therefore in direct touch with the managers who make the overall decisions and do not have to try to decode them after they have passed through a series of intervening minds that may not have fully appreciated their implications and emphases. In the same way, the heads of cells are in direct touch with the employees doing the work on the shop floor or in the field, directly in charge of them and responsible for them, and so can pass on any significant information straight to the command group. And by their direct contact with that group they are much better able to realize what information is significant.

2. *It facilitates lateral communication.* Hierarchical corporations are often riddled with prohibitions and inhibitions about who can write or talk to whom without a long bureaucratic journey of permission up one side of the hierarchy, across one of the great divides, and down the other side. In a cell system it is much easier for a member of a marketing cell, say, to stroll over and chat with someone in the research labs or on the production floor. This is almost always fruitful of knowledge, understanding, and ideas; the prohibitions and inhibitions nearly always act against the interest of the corporation as a whole, though they are very much in the sectional interest of departmental barons whose careers are built on a policy of *suppressio veri* interspersed with bouts of *suggestio falsi.*

3. *It liberates the spirit.* I once had to deal more or less at the same time with two large companies, both of them in the same line of business. One was well and firmly managed, highly profitable, well planned, and extremely efficient. The other was going through a palace revolution, had been

badly managed for a long period, had some good products but also some that were out of date, and was only marginally profitable. I had no doubt which was the one to invest in, and yet I would ten times rather have worked in the other. The first was just boring. Everyone had a sensibly set target that could be achieved by hard work; they were all well paid; they had no complaint about the management, but the whole place had a dead sort of feeling.

The inefficient company, however, was an exciting and lively place. People were toying with new ideas for products that were not really their job to think about, they argued about the way things were done, they criticized management decisions, they took decisions on their own responsibility which they should have referred up, but they were more alive, they were fuller people. Not all of them of course, and they had at least their fair share of the dull and unenterprising; but it was a stimulating firm to be with. There is no moral to this story, since the efficient firm is likely to pay a good return on capital for many years and the inefficient one may not survive. But the efficient firm may yet be heading for dangerous rigidity, and excluding the really bright individuals. A friend of mine used to say that the bigger the organization, the fewer the jobs worth doing, and it also seems to be true, to judge from the second firm, that the bigger the disorganization the more jobs worth doing. But the cell structure is the best hope of combining the spirit of the second organization with the profitability of the first.

4. *It aims at success through diversity rather than success through conformity.* Instead of a unified hierarchy with all the top people reinforcing each other's prejudices, there are a number of nearly autonomous cells each led by managers with different attitudes and emphases. It is the difference

between the closed society and the liberal society; a closed society like Ming China or nineteenth- and twentieth-century England or the France of Louis XIV and XV, and a liberal society like the United States. It is the closed society that fails to meet change, that becomes cut off from reality, that does not see the way things are going and that ultimately crashes; it is the open society, where the highest levels are open to anyone, and not to a limited group or class, that can change and adapt with events. And so when radical change comes, the cell-structure company is likely to have at least some cells that recognize it quickly and are able to cash in on it. They become the new growth areas, their profitability makes up for the decline of others, they wield the influence and make the important decisions for the future, and the company incorporates the revolution and rides it, instead of resisting it and being crushed by it.

Although you can draw a cell structure on paper—it is simply a number of circles, perhaps of different sizes, linked to a central circle—it is much more of an attitude of mind than a diagram. Many managers who would draw their organization as a conventional genealogical hierarchy are in fact operating something very close to a cell system. The hierarchical attitude is revealed in phrases like, "This memo must go through me," "I must be notified before one of your staff comes here," "If you want to talk to my subordinate then I must be present"; the cell attitude, in phrases like, "Why don't you go and put it to him yourself?" "You don't need me at this meeting do you?" "Come back to me if you need some more ammunition," "Perhaps you'd better drop over and have a word with the marketing boys?" The difference is a difference of security as against insecurity.

In a hierarchy, most managers are kept from those on whose opinion their reputation ultimately rests by layers of senior managers. They therefore feel they are being judged on the basis of what can be discovered about them from memos and minutes or said about them by superiors. This makes them sticklers for appearances, since they are judged by appearances; they suspect that all knowledge about their operations will be used as evidence against them, and the sight of one of their subordinates talking to the boss sets their ulcer twitching. In a cell system there are no insulating layers, the boss or his central-cell cabinet talk directly to all the heads of cells and many of their deputies, and most managers feel they are known and judged for the results they achieve rather than as they are represented to be by others or appear to be from various pieces of paper.

In writing about the cell structure it is difficult not to appear to be advocating it for all large firms, when in fact it is not suitable for all of them; but one of the great problems of managing large corporations is to gain the financial advantages of being large without losing the administrative advantages of being small. And one of the best ways of doing this is to erase the hierarchical pattern from the minds of managers—or at least to inscribe next to it the cells and the central cell, the monastery and the headquarters of the order, the colonies and the mother country, as a possible alternative.

# 10

## THE CREATIVE MANAGER

It is too late to change it now, but "manager" is an insulting and belittling word. It carries a sense of someone put in by the owner to keep the thing going while he is not there. "Director" has a ring of opulence, even "worker" has an unpretentious dignity, but "manager" sounds dangerously like a euphemism for foreman. He is neither a thinker nor a doer, he is just a manager. I suppose it dates back to a time when he really was just a manager: The mill owner or mine owner wanted a simple and unvarying process to be continued indefinitely in more places than he could supervise personally, so he hired someone who could manage in his absence, someone drawn from the social class of the workers to discharge the more disagreeable tasks of the employer.

Of course, words can outgrow their base origins; but sometimes those who are designated by them use them as a refuge and perpetuate the slightly pejorative connotation. "Administrator" has been a good case of this: Officials in the civil service and the big corporations have hidden behind it for many years, and used "administration" as a mystique to justify drawing a leadership-size salary without exercising a function of leadership. Now there seems to be a danger that managers are hiding behind the word "management" in order to fend off the idea of creativeness. It is, of course, undoubtedly true that the word creativeness is also gaining an undesirable connotation. Long-haired, clever, irresponsible; people the manager has to manage very tactfully, because they are difficult to organize, temperamental, and yet in some way necessary, even indispensable. They are a sort of colony of licensed eccentrics: "I'll get the creative boys to kick it around," "This is what the creative chaps have come up with," "He's a very good guy really, but...well, you know what these creative people are." The manager finds it thoroughly unsatisfactory that the future of the whole business should rest, as it apparently does, on such an unpredictable and volatile foundation. He, however, has the title of manager. No taint of creativeness about that; and it is a good word to fend off any suggestion that perhaps he ought to be creative himself.

The manager, of course, unlike the administrator, would not resist the title of leader: group leader, team leader, project leader, are perfectly acceptable terms. It may frighten "administrators," but a lot of managers accept the idea of being a boss quite happily. And yet leadership, especially at the highest levels, is becoming more and more concerned with change. The days are over when a firm could continue profitably for three generations casting toilet tanks, baths, and manhole covers from the same three hallowed molds. Change has become the dominant concern of top management, and growth plans are geared to projected changes in wealth, technology, demand patterns, birthrate, habit, taste, population distribution, power supply, raw material production, and other such considerations. As these factors change, so the firm's activities must change to meet them; and change can be of only two kinds—imitative or creative. You can change the way other people have changed already, or you can change in a new way. You can follow, or you can lead. You can wait until you find out how other firms have coped with or exploited the projected changes, and then copy them, or you can think up original ideas that they have not hit on. And if you do that, you are being creative in the fullest sense. Change is not a sideline in the business of leadership, it is integral to the whole idea: to describe someone who left things exactly as he found them as a "great leader" would be a contradiction in terms. A leader may change the map of Europe, or the breakfast habits of a nation, or the capital structure of an engineering corporation; but changing things is central to leadership, and changing them before anyone else is creativeness.

It is strange and quite illogical that creativeness should, in the public mind, be linked to long hair and dirty fingernails instead of gray flannel suits and pin-stripe trousers. It is not a rare human attribute like telepathy or double-jointed knees; it is quite a normal quality like intelligence or manual skill, which most children possess in some degree, as any teacher of five-year-olds will tell you. If most teachers of eighteen-year-olds would question it, that is a reflection on our method of education, not on children. A great many managers are in fact creative people, but people are liable to balk at the idea because they do not look like painters or poets. Nor do most good painters and poets, for that matter, but there is a pre-Raphaelite stereotype that creative people are expected to conform to. Arthur Koestler in the *Act of Creation*[1] explains creativeness as the result of bisociation, of putting together two unconnected facts or ideas to form a single new idea. Of course it is an ingredient of great art, if handled by a great artist. The two unconnected ideas of one army beating another and placing its banner where the enemy's once stood, and the pallor of death draining the blood from the face of a dying woman, are united creatively by Shakespeare into:

Thou art not conquered; beauty's ensign yet
Is crimson in thy lips and in thy cheeks,
And death's pale flag is not advanced there.[2]

Equally, this bisociation can lead to a discovery, as when
Newton saw an apple fall in an orchard when pondering
the anomalies in the orbits of planets, and hit on gravita-
tional theory and the attraction of masses. Or it can lead to
an invention—Koestler[3] quotes the case of Gutenberg puzzling over ways of reproducing the written word while
watching the grapes being pressed, and suddenly seeing
the printing press as the answer.

All these are spectacular examples of creativeness, and
few of the creative ideas of managers are likely to win such
enduring fame. But in a small way creative ideas are being
produced all the time. Take the simple problem of the
movie parking lot: A reasonable charge is seventy-five
cents per car, but the management wants to encourage
patrons by charging them only fifty cents. How can you tell
which motorists are bona fide patrons? Follow them all in?
Ask them, but don't believe the shifty ones? The answer
devised by a creative manager was to charge everyone
seventy-five cents and give them a ticket that was a
voucher for the first twenty-five cents of the cost of their
seat for that performance. It may not rank with Shakespeare and Newton, but it is no less creative for that.

The universal nature of creativeness became particularly clear to me when I left television and worked on a
project that demanded close study of an engineering factory. Television has the reputation of being full of creative
people, and engineering has not. And yet after a week or
two it suddenly dawned on me that a television program
and an engineering product went through a virtually identical process and demanded almost exactly the same qualities from the people responsible for them. The design

engineer is told in broad terms what is wanted: a simple, light-motor mower for the smaller lawn, costing between $75 and $90, and selling at a rate of about two hundred a week. So is the television writer or producer: a thirty-minute twice-weekly thriller serial for the 6:30 P.M.-7:00 P.M. spot for an audience of 10 to 15 percent on a budget of $400,000 a week. The engineer and scriptwriter both go away, read a bit, talk the subject around, perhaps check back on a few points, and finally come up with a document. If the document looks promising, the engineer is told to go and make a lab model, and the producer and scriptwriter to do a pilot program. If these are successful, they both pose the same problem: It is all very well to prove that these clever individuals, given lots of time and facilities and strong incentive, can produce just one program/model that works—but can the staff in the television studio and the operatives on the factory floor produce them to the same quality at a steady rate within the agreed budget? So the factory goes into production development and the television company commissions an initial series of six, during which time certain snags are worked out and changes are made that make conveyor-belt production easier.

Of course, there were wide differences in the backgrounds and knowledge and skills of the people involved, but the creative demands are just the same; yet somehow people who are verbally creative are licensed to be "creative people" while those who are mathematically and mechanically creative are not. And, of course, just as some managers hide behind the word "manager" to evade the responsibility of creativeness, so some creative people hide behind the word "creativeness" as an excuse for overspending their budgets, not delivering on time, and never being available when wanted. But it is by no means necessarily the best of them who do this, and in my experience efficiency is as much a part of the best creative people as creativeness is of the best managers. Those who flaunt their creativeness to conceal their laziness ought to have their poetic licenses revoked.

The most important act of creativeness, however, in the case of both the lawn mower and the television program, was the one that was taken before the engineer and the scriptwriter began: the idea that there was a need for this product and a profit to be made by supplying it. If that idea was wrong, then however good the subsequent creative ideas the product will fail. And the person responsible for that idea is the manager—the creative manager. This is not to say that he has to have all the ideas himself, or even most of them. But to deal in an area where so much depends on creativeness he must keep his own creative faculties alert. Even the act of deciding between proposed alternatives is creative. It does not have to be: There are creative and uncreative ways of making decisions. A simple case is the picture editor who wants a picture of Times Square to illustrate a feature article or news story. When forty are brought up from the picture library, the uncreative mind selects the most suitable. The creative mind, however, first of all creates its own mental picture of the sort of feeling and atmosphere and information the picture should convey, and then looks through the forty library pictures to see if one of them is right. It may be that several are, but it may be that none are, in which case she will reject the lot and dispatch a staff photographer or send out to the agencies. Or take the dry cleaning firm ordering a fleet of delivery vans. Because they carry evening dresses on hangers, they need a minimum interior clearance of five feet. The uncreative mind examines a range of such vans and picks the one that is best for the job: But the creative mind has a picture of what it wants, and that does not include the expensive width and engine size that go with that size interior clearance. It wants a small, light, narrow delivery wagon, but five feet high, and it gets the vehicle manufacturers to build a simple raised roof on its cheapest van for a net saving of several thousand dollars capital outlay, and rather more in fuel, maintenance, garaging, tax, and depreciation.

It is in the consideration of proposals put up by others that managers most often have to exercise creativeness. The uncreative manager examines a proposal on its own terms—he may question the solution proposed, but not the overall problem to which it offers a solution. The creative manager thinks creatively about the nature of the problem before reading the document, and formulates one or two elements that any solution must embody. He may then find that although the proposed solution is reasonable and internally consistent, a part of the problem has been ducked or overlooked. The uncreative mind can spot wrong answers, but it takes a creative mind to spot wrong questions. This is particularly important because of the nature of many corporation proposal-type documents. I have both written and received a fair number of these myself, and I know that the real skill in writing them lies not in finding a solution to your problem, but in finding a problem to your solution. The solution is easy: It is a list of all the means by which you want to increase your own power and status and freedom and security while shedding uncongenial work and unwelcome responsibility. The skill lies in making it appear that all these are merely the inevitable steps toward the solution of a genuine and pressing problem that concerns the whole department or the whole company.

Another invaluable device is the phony alternative: "Either we must accept a reduced rate of growth, or we must greatly expand the responsibilities of the marketing division." The creative mind at once starts to think up a few more unstated alternatives; the uncreative mind is liable to walk straight into the trap.

Few managers would deny the need for this sort of judgment, this sort of attitude, but if you accused them of being creative they would suspect you were equating them with a temperamental copywriter or an effeminate art director. And yet historians talk quite naturally about creative statesmen—it is the term A.J.P. Taylor applies to Churchill and Lloyd George. Perhaps if we can look upon creativeness not as a mutational freak but a normal ingredient of a balanced personality we may one day be able to call a manager creative without offense—perhaps even as a compliment.

# 11

## CREATIVE INTERCOURSE

Creativeness in industry has never been unimportant, but it has never been as important as it is now. The reason is quite simple: the pace of change. For the industrialist, the manager, there are two areas in which change dominates his thinking: the technology and the market, what he can produce and what people want to buy—supply and demand. Technological advance is constantly bringing new possibilities into his range: either new techniques and processes and tools and materials, or old ones at new low prices that make it possible to use them on new products. And customer demand is also constantly changing, as people become wealthier and can afford new products, or as technological advance brings older or better ones within their range. There comes a point, for instance, as the cost of plastic pressings comes down and the cost of labor and transport goes up, when it becomes cheaper to distribute milk in disposable plastic cartons than in returnable glass bottles. There comes a point, as the cost of sound recording equipment goes down and the market expenditure per head on video equipment goes up, when it becomes profitable to put video equipment with synchronous sound on to the general market. There comes a point, as British printing costs rise and European freight costs fall, when it becomes cheaper to print illustrated English books in Czechoslovakia than in England. Yes, but someone has got to think of it. It is obvious enough when you state the two relevant facts and no others, but for the people in the industry they are only two out of thousands of facts they are aware of. To put the two together and launch a new product or cut the price of an old one requires an act of bisociation, a creative act; and a creative act demands a creative person.

It is obviously important, therefore, to understand how creative people work best, how a steady supply of good new ideas can be generated. Although the popular picture is of a single creative person, the painter alone in his studio or the poet alone in his garret, in fact two are needed, male and female, father and mother. To posterity, the Medici tomb in Florence is the unaided work of Michelangelo; but before he started work he engaged in prolonged discussion and exchanged some fifty letters with the patron, the man who commissioned it, Pope Clement VII. And these discussions were about important practical matters—the size, the subject, the characters, the general design, and so on. Edgar Wind[1] points out that although there is a time when an artist needs to be left alone without interruption in order to produce his work of art, there is a time before that when he very much wants ideas, facts, guidance, and practical suggestions. In the case of the Medici tomb this was provided by Clement VII, who acted as father to it, while Michelangelo was the mother. (Few of the wealthy companies that commission frescoes and sculptures for their new buildings realize that patronage is something more than signing checks made out to established artists, which is why so many imposing buildings have such strange, arid, irrelevant pieces of stone or metal stuck in front of them.) It is true that few industries employ Clement VIIs and Michelangelos, but they need the same creative coupling to produce their new designs and plans.

The process is, in fact, almost uncomfortably similar to sexual intercourse. The male, the father, say the product planning manager, has the seed of the idea, and he sends for the special projects designer. The meeting starts to stimulate both of them; after some preliminary talking around the subject, they come together with the same idea, and the excitement rises until the seed of the idea is transferred from the male and accepted by the female, and they both relax in a state of euphoric creative exhaustion and go off for a drink. But already the idea is starting to grow and develop inside the female, in the designer's mind. She goes away and fosters it while the male, the creative manager, makes sure the necessary nourishment and protection and secure environment are provided until the brainchild is born. It is still a child, though, and the father has to see it is properly trained and disciplined while the mother goes on seeing to its growth and nourishment, until finally it is a product in the shops and they can leave it to make its own way in the world.

Perhaps I ought to point out quickly that the parallel is a parallel of processes only, not of natures. There is no suggestion that someone who develops an idea implanted by someone else is effeminate. On the contrary, it is those who are best able to receive ideas who are also best able to implant them. The creative process always works both ways, and someone who receives a creative idea implanted by one person very often has to go off and fertilize several other creative people before the product can be brought forth. And of course there is no creative monogamy in industry—one male can fertilize a number of females, and there certainly are creative stallions, including some of the best creative managers, who play the male role much more than the female. The trouble is that since the mare's part in producing the offspring is obvious to all in the company, the stallion's role may not be properly understood or appreciated by those in charge. They may eventually notice that when the mare is put to another stallion, when the designer goes and works in another department, the offspring do not win races anymore. In my experience the stallions of industry are undervalued—look at the comparative prices fetched by stallions and mares at thoroughbred sales. There are other lessons, too: Do not, for instance, put two stallions in the same field of mares if you want to avoid trouble. And if you want a certain kind of offspring, cross the right male with the right female. If you are designing trucks for the Middle East, make the designer talk to the Middle Eastern sales manager before he retires to the drawing board.

Of course, not every mating results in conception, even when no steps are being taken to prevent it. And even when it does take place there will sometimes be stillbirths and deformed children, as well as occasional abortions. Much will depend on eugenic factors, on the quality of the stallion and the mare; but much also depends on why the decision was taken to have a child at all. To meet change, certainly; but what sort of change supplied the impulse for the decision?

There are two ways of looking for a new idea: inward or outward, at what you can make or at what people want, at your supply or their demand. It may seem obvious to say that good products have to be demand-oriented, they have to spring from what people want and not what you can make; certainly no one would start up a new manufacturing company of his own without being convinced that people would buy what he intended to produce. However, it is not new companies that are in danger of the heresy of supply-orientation, it is the old ones. The classic case is the English cotton industry, which nearly destroyed itself by thinking in terms of what it supplied. "We spin and weave cotton" was their dominant thought, and all ideas had to spring from there—they had to be ideas for selling the cotton the factories were producing. But "we spin and weave cotton" is a statement produced by looking inward, by being preoccupied with looms and spindles. They left others to develop the new technologies of circular knitting and synthetic fibers. If they had looked outward, at their market, they would have come up with a different statement, namely, "People wear clothes." In that case they would have been integrating with knitted goods and synthetic fibers from the start, instead of desperately diversifying into brick making and cake shops at the finish.

One of the best instances of starting from the market and not the factory is the Prussian war against Austria. Bismarck did not say, "There's my army, now what can I do with it to make Prussia as great a power as Austria?" He started the other way round, decided that uniting the North German states under Prussia would achieve the object, and that victory over Austria would be a necessary preliminary. Then having determined what the market required, he consulted his production manager about the possibility of turning out the product; or, to be more precise, he asked General von Moltke if it could be done. Moltke said that with France neutral and Prussia in alliance with Italy it could; Bismarck negotiated both conditions, and von Moltke met his schedule. In other words, the demand was accepted as the datum, and the supply was altered to fit it. Clearly, the good idea, even though it starts in the marketplace, must be one that the factory can produce, just as the bad idea, even though it starts in the factory, will be for a product that some people might buy. The question is: Which do you treat as unalterable and which as flexible? Do you say, "Well, we can't go altering our plant, so let's try to persuade people to buy this," or "Well, people certainly would like this, so let's set about making it"?

Obviously, if there is a lack of connection between supply and demand you have to alter one to fit the other. The trouble is that altering the supply requires a great deal of thought and work and risk. It may mean reequipping factories, retraining a sales force, setting up a new research group, market testing, recruitment, and a lot of other complicated and laborious activities. That is why the prospect of altering the demand to fit the supply is so seductive, and a great section of the advertising industry thrives on implying that this can be the solution. Certainly advertising can link a supply to a demand, probably it can awake a latent demand, but there is no evidence that it can create a demand that is not there. The other way of altering demand has been noted and described by John Kenneth Galbraith,[2] Vance Packard,[3] and others: change the styling, the coloring, the packaging; build in the obsolescence factor either structurally or in taste and fashion. This enables you to keep your plant and suppliers churning out the same products while you only have to reorganize the paint shop. Apparently this works, at least for a time; but there is another way, the way of changing what you supply. A Swedish cigar factory that was hit by a slump in cigar sales might have put large sums into cigar advertising to try to revive the slackening demand. Instead they put a smaller sum into an ingenious conversion of their factory into a herring-gutting plant, for which there was a rising demand.

Perhaps the most valuable of all qualities in the creative manager is the ability to locate the hidden demand, to think of something people have not got but would like, and which his firm could make at a price they would pay.

Market research is not much use for this: People may be able to talk critically and comparatively about things they have used, but they cannot talk creatively about things that have not been thought of. Certainly, in television program research, the question "What sort of program would you like to see?" got exactly the same answer as "What sort of program have you enjoyed in the past?" To think up this kind of idea, you need to discover the want in yourself. Noel Coward's recipe for pleasing audiences was straightforward and simple: Write what pleases you, and if it doesn't please the audience get out of the business fast. All managers are consumers too—the auto firm is managed by men who are also motorists, the shoe firm by people who walk, the restaurant chain by people who go out for meals. The secret is to discover the consumer in oneself and think imaginatively about what he would like and has not got. The television producer is the first viewer of his program— he sees it go past in his mind's eye before anyone else can look at it. The dispassionate calculation of probable success or failure based on no personal feelings but just the market research figures and past records may provide safety at times, but very rarely a winner. It is true that the consumer in oneself may have tastes that are unrepresentative, but part of learning the business consists in filtering out the elements that differ from those of most consumers and leaving in the ones that are true to the general taste.

There is another aspect of a corporation in which constant change demands constant creative reassessment: its own internal arrangements for producing what it needs with what it has got. Departmental structures, routine meetings, standard documents and procedures have a way of taking on a life of their own. They may have been right for the intake of raw material and distribution of factories and marketing practices, and the range and balance of products that existed when they were set up; but all these may change, and yet the organization, the meetings, the standard returns of facts and figures may well remain unchanged and become more and more of a drag on the work. There is a good game called "Starting from Scratch" in which management asks itself how it would organize its current production given its current resources and nothing else. You have to produce so much a week, and here are your factories and your capital. Organize them. The results can be illuminating, even if they only make people face truths that they had been concealing from themselves. One big British chain store has an attitude of looking at all their internal organization and asking, "Why should we keep it?" It is a more creative question than, "Why should we change it?"

There is a story that the Royal Artillery were giving a demonstration to some visiting Europeans on Salisbury plain in the 1950s. The visitors were most impressed with the speed and precision of the light artillery crew, but one of them asked what was the duty of the man who stood at attention throughout the whole demonstration.

"He's number six," the adjutant explained.

"I too can count. But why is he there?"

"That's his job. Number six stands at attention throughout."

"But why then do you not have five?"

No one knew. It took a great deal of research through old training manuals, but finally they discovered his duty.

He was the one who held the horses.

# 12

## *EDUCATING FOR CREATIVENESS*

We are only just moving out of the era when something like 80 percent of the people employed in agriculture, manufacturing, and raw material production are asked to give nothing more during their working lives than their time, their muscles, and a tiny part of their minds: routine clerical jobs in the offices and routine physical jobs in the fields and mines and on the shop floor. It is quite possible that future generations will look back on the conditions of labor in the first half of the twentieth century with the same sort of incredulous horror with which we today look back on the child workers in the early years of the nineteenth. The mopping up of routine, deadening work by computers, transfer machines, mechanized mining and agriculture, and computer-controlled machine-tool centers may turn out to be as profound, if not as personal, a benefaction as all the ameliorative labor legislation of the past century. Of course, some routine work will remain, just as there was some mentally stimulating work before, but the emphasis is clearly moving right over.

One result of this shift will be to reveal with much greater clarity the qualities on which industrial success depends. Initiative and drive and originality and creativeness will stand out like the bones of a skeleton when the flesh has been stripped away, as the characteristics that are still needed as much as, or more than, ever before. Above all, I suspect, originality and creativeness. The routine staff,

the clerical workers and unskilled and semiskilled opera-
tors, will no longer be there to act as a bottom layer who
enable the people above them to seem to be doing useful
management work by simply handling the problems, like
leave and sickness and grievances, that a large number of
people are bound to generate. This is not a particularly
horrifying prospect, since there is a tremendous pool of
unused creative ability that at the moment finds its satisfaction outside work in home decorating and carpentry
and model making and car tuning, and which, if employed
at work, would make the job far more satisfying for the
person doing it as well as giving better value to the employer. You can see this even at the top level—the British
civil servant with an honors degree who does the *Times*
crossword puzzle each day because it is the only testing
intellectual challenge he gets in a job that may fully occupy
his time quantitatively, but not qualitatively, in that it
rarely engages the best part of his mind.

Just how much originality and creativeness you can
find if you need it and can pay for it can be seen in the
enormous postwar growth of computers and television
and advertising and design and popular music. Before the
war they only employed a tiny proportion of their present
numbers. This cannot be owing to a new breed of creative
people; it is simply that these new careers have provided
outlets for the creative abilities of the present generation
which were repressed and unrealized in their parents. I
would say that, by comparison, industry does not provide
enough outlets for the creativeness of engineers. The exceptions, like the electric toothbrush, do more to show the
range of possibilities than disprove the point. After all, the
electric toothbrush could have been produced ages earlier;
it did not need any technological breakthrough, only an
original idea from an inventive engineering mind. In the

end, a large number of manufacturers fall back on the creativeness of advertisers to try to provide some spurious emotional differentiation of a product that is otherwise indistinguishable from its competitors. I have never understood why so many firms use outside advertising agencies; I should have thought that the most fruitful time to employ the advertisers' skills would be at the beginning, so that the desirable and appetizing qualities that they specialize in applying could be built into the product instead of the commercials.

If the routine jobs are constantly decreasing and the jobs requiring creativeness are increasing, then clearly a burden falls on the educational system—the burden of sending children out to earn their living equipped with original, creative, and inquiring minds in addition to the high level of knowledge that, in the sciences at least, will also be a prerequisite. It is in this area that the British educational system (with only very few honorable exceptions) seems to me to be failing more spectacularly than in any other. Not in the early stages: The influence of educational theorists like Friedrich Froebel, Maria Montessori, and Johann Pestalozzi makes sure that creativeness and originality are encouraged and liberated in the first years of primary education; it is when shades of the examination room begin to close upon the growing boy and girl that the trouble starts. This was brought home to me with depressing force when I had to interview a large number of candidates, over several months, for vacancies in television production. Most of them had been through school and college, the majority with some success. They were reasonably polite, and, I presume, quite knowledgeable in their subjects. What was missing from nearly all of them was any spark of originality, any creative ideas, any radical criticism, any urge to do something new or different. Yes, they watched television programs. Yes, they were very good. Yes, they'd like to work on them. Well, no, they hadn't really thought of anything special they'd like to do. No, they hadn't really any criticisms of the programs they'd watched. No, they didn't think there were any kinds of programs not being done that ought to be. No, they didn't think there was too much of any particular kind of program. Well, they just wanted to work on a program like X or Y. No, they didn't really know what that would involve, but presumably someone would tell them.

These, I repeat, were graduates, mostly with good degrees, mostly from respected universities. It was fairly clear what had happened: From the moment they were singled out as the academic elite, all their originality and creativeness were ignored or repressed. In history or English, no one wanted to hear their own immature and probably ill-founded opinions and interpretations and comments, they wanted to find out how well they could digest and reproduce the standard judgments of maturer minds. No one wanted to know what they thought about *Hamlet,* they wanted to know if they knew what noted critics, scholars, and interpreters had said. Originality and creativeness are not unquenchable flames, except in a few highly creative people. In many cases they are all too quenchable, and, if you spend ten years pouring the accumulated wisdom of the ages over them, it is hardly surprising if they go out. And added to this was the terrible attitude of mind that the examination system fosters; the attitude of waiting to be told what to do next, to be given a precise syllabus, a curriculum, an examination date, and someone to make sure they follow the first leading to the second until they reach the third. For ten years they are conditioned to a steeplechase way of life: a series of fences labeled first grade, second grade through to eighth or ninth grade, high school exams, college entrance boards, degrees, with a jockey riding them all the time. It is hardly surprising if they emerge with no ideas of their own about what they want to do, but simply waiting for another jockey to ride them at another fence. When it dawns on them that there are no jockeys, and it is their job to build the sort of fence they want, they look baffled and faintly cheated.

An examination, after all, is not a phenomenon that is much in evidence once the days of education are over. Probably one of the few school activities that bears any real resemblance to working life is the school play, a project requiring thought, preparation, and work, that involves people of all sorts of different skills and abilities, that gradually develops and takes shape by a certain date on which it has to be ready for presentation to the public. It also imposes the same interdependence: Suddenly the hidden skills of the children who can build scenery or design costumes or list and supply props or make lights fade come to be important and respected; and, as in an industrial project, failure lurks in the background—lights fusing, scenery collapsing, lines forgotten.

It is true that there is another educational practice that incorporates the advantages of a school play, namely, education by group project, where all the class, or all the school, have to find out about, say, life in their city a hundred years ago: The engineers reconstruct models of old industrial machinery, the photographers and artists record what still remains and collect old photos and drawings, the carpenters build models of the old city center, the literary ones produce a book about different aspects of life then, the historians find out about events and personalities of the time, and the whole exhibition is brought together for display to parents and local people who are interested. This is a demanding and rewarding kind of work for the practical, and for the academic carries the tremendous stimulus of discovering and collating new knowledge instead of just trying to catch up on a tiny portion of what others have discovered and recorded already. The trouble is that this sort of study is in fact considered much too frivolous, much too much of a luxury, for the clever children. They have the examinations to think about.

The examinations. Over the years they have grown from a useful check on what the pupils have been doing into a rigid schedule of what they must learn, however boring they may find it or however eager they may be to learn other things, and the yardstick by which schools and colleges measure their own success or failure. Schools measure their success in SAT scores and university admissions, and teachers by the number of degrees their students earn. What happens after that is not their concern. Few educators are enamored of the system, but hardly anyone is prepared to change it. It is the classic case of altering the demand to fit the supply, of refusing to change the product and trying to change the market instead. And since there is no competition, the system is perpetuated. There are deviants and experiments—York University has a paper that the undergraduates have two weeks to write, consulting whatever sources they choose. It is a beginning. But for the most part, industry is presented with an annual output of graduates carefully trained for uncreativeness.

The irony is that if the graduates were asked why they wanted a degree at all, most of them would say, "In order to get a good job." It would be interesting if one of the new corporation-states were to bypass the system. Education, after all, is a function of advanced states, and strong pressure for universal education in the 1860s came from employers who needed literate employees. Suppose a giant corporation were to guarantee university places and a wide choice of jobs at high starting salaries to a group of bright fourteen-year-olds—the jobs to be taken up when they were twenty-one. Then they could play "starting from scratch"—they could construct a syllabus that certainly instructed them in the necessary disciplines and gave them the requisite background knowledge, but that also forced them to do original work, have original ideas, devise research projects and plan and coordinate the work of others, take the lead in projects, and in fact start doing as intellectual exercise and training the kind of work they would be called on to do when they left the university and entered the corporation. It would, of course, be academic, and supervised by academic people. But it would emphasize creativeness and originality and initiative as much as memory and intelligence and examination technique. There must be many people in industry and education who would be delighted to shake off the shackles of examinations and plan a course of real education from the age of fourteen to twenty-one. Perhaps one day they will have a chance. Perhaps one day we will stop educating for conformity and start educating for creativeness.

# 13

## CREATIVE GROUPS

Despite the importance of creativeness in industry, it would be foolish and dangerous to assume that it is the only desirable quality, or that the ideal firm would consist exclusively of creative people. Today's success usually comes from yesterday's creativeness, and there will always be a need for the efficient manager of a going concern who has no original ideas to contribute, but who can keep things running happily and profitably once they have been devised and started. This is the kind of manager for whom the vast majority of the management books are written, and I have nothing to add. Indeed, the need is not for addition but subtraction. However, the top management of a firm should be concerned about tomorrow's success—on the night before Alamein, Montgomery was thinking hard about the invasion of Sicily—and tomorrow's success comes from today's creativeness. It is therefore important to know if you can arrange for the right sort of creativeness to happen, or if you just have to try to recruit the right sort of people and then cross your fingers and pray.

Perhaps one day it will be possible to formulate scientific laws for the generating of creative ideas, but that day has not yet come. Nevertheless, if you look back on a number of creative movements, there is one pattern that seems to repeat itself, the pattern of a leader who is himself a highly creative person working with a small nucleus around him, a creative group. It is by no means the only way to bring about change, or to seize and fashion to your own ends change that is happening, but it seems to have been consistently successful. There are numerous examples ranging from Charlemagne and Henry II to Lenin and Margaret Thatcher. Sometimes, if the group is successful, it may grow until it appears to be very large; but if you look closely you find that only a small number belong to the central nucleus, however much power and responsibility other people may have in particular but limited areas of the enterprise. Groups of this same kind can be found in art, in science, in military history, in social reform, and other areas of life. They also happen in industry; not all that often in my experience, but if you have ever worked in or close to one, you recognize others at once; and if you observe them and talk to people inside and outside them, you find they share a number of important characteristics that also seem to have been shared by the creative groups of the past.

1. *The authority of the leader is unquestioned and unchallenged.* In fact, in a successful group the leader is often spoken of with an uncritical admiration that borders on reverence and infuriates outsiders. Just what makes a creative leader is so important that it must be dealt with separately; for the moment it is sufficient to say that without one the creative group does not exist. He is the stallion; there must also be his mares, though they themselves may become stallions (substallions?) so to speak, when with their own subordinates. Obviously you cannot lay down an exact number for this group, but I would be surprised to find a leader with more than five people who formed the central nucleus and I would think that three is closer to the norm; this is not to say that there cannot be many more trusted and able

members of the group—only that the central nucleus must be small.

2. *Within the central nucleus there is dialogue.* This is a difficult concept to describe to those who have not experienced it, but an important one. It seems to be the product of long thrashing-out sessions—call them debates or discussions if you prefer, but they are usually very informal—at which attitudes, ideas, policies, and critical standards are hammered out until there is a body of shared convictions about methods and products and markets or whatever the group's business is concerned with. The emotional impulse is usually dissatisfaction with what is being done, or not being done, by other people in the business; this of course happens outside creative groups as well, and the distinguishing factor of a creative group is that it produces a positive, constructive, and original idea. It may be a bad idea, but it is an idea and not just an anthology of gripes. And once this is hammered out, over the months, it forms a basis for a continuing dialogue, discussions that rest on such a broad base of shared convictions that they usually end with agreement, improved understanding of the group's business (or art), perhaps new ideas to investigate or develop, and a broader base for further dialogue. This makes it difficult for newcomers to reach the central nucleus, since there are so many shared convictions that in time become underlying assumptions and often take a lot of discovering. It also tends to make the group unpopular with people outside it, since they nearly always side with each other in argument and appear deliberately exclusive.

3. *Creative groups need output.* They do not work at their best when spirited away to a country house and told to "have some ideas." It is not remarkable that Shakespeare wrote his plays while he was an active member of the Lord

Chamberlain's players; it is exactly what you would expect. They were a creative group (led by Richard Burbage) from which a considerable output was demanded in the shape of new productions for new occasions, and the group's success, as so often happens, was in proportion not only to the qualities of its members but also to the demands made upon it. Any creative group belongs where the work is being done, in the blast furnace of ideas, on the assembly line of thought.

Output is necessary in the first instance as a spur to ideas: The knowledge that a deadline is approaching, that something has to be done urgently, is a wonderful liberator of the creative impulse. That is why the "wastage" principle does not work with creative groups. The idea of getting ten groups all to put in an idea from which one will be selected and nine discarded does not get the best out of these groups: The sense of urgency is divided by ten. Much better, very often, is for the one group to bear the responsibility alone, to know that everything depends on what it comes up with, and that good or bad, the result will go into production because there is nothing else. Leonidas and his Spartans would not have fought so bravely at Thermopylae if they had known that there were nine more regiments from other cities waiting in reserve.

Output is also important for morale. Creative groups use up a lot of energy. Often they work hard and long and late, and they cannot be supervised, checked on for punctuality and efficiency, as the more routine performers can. It is often impossible anyway, but when morale is high it is also unnecessary because the work becomes a great source of satisfaction. For this reason, they respond better to encouragement and enthusiasm than many others do. But most of all they respond to success, to the visible, objective success of what they are doing. This is the only real morale raiser, and since high morale is vital to a successful creative group, a regular, indeed an exceptionally high, demand on their output is vital as well.

The third need for output is as feedback. If the dialogue is to continue, then there must be a continuous supply of new data, a continuous learning process. Only by continuing to produce can improvements be made, new facts revealed, and the body of shared convictions augmented or revised or refined by new evidence.

4. *The leader of a creative group must have as much autonomy as possible.* He must be able to implement the ideas of the group on his own responsibility. If they have to be passed up to someone else, they will not be put into effect with the same understanding, nor with the same confidence and enthusiasm. And, of course, the group works with all the more willingness if it knows that the leader is the one who will actually implement the idea himself and not just go off and try to sell it to someone else.

5. *Creative groups have to grow, or they die.* If they devise and launch a new and successful project, they are unlikely to be satisfied with the running of it once it is established. Indeed, the mere fact of being good enough to launch it is proof that they are too good to run it—at least as a full-time job. They need the constant stimulus of bigger challenges and responsibilities, better resources, larger budget, more staff, as well as sufficient personal promotion and increase of salary to keep their morale high. Given this, they seem to be able to go on for a very long time, perhaps growing from a small section into a department and then into a division or a subsidiary company, and perhaps finally becoming the management group of the corporation.

It is an attractive idea to think that the members of a creative group can be removed and turned into creative leaders with groups of their own. It does not seem to work. They can make good executives, but it seems that the simple fact that they work well under a creative leader is evidence that they are not creative leaders themselves. There are, however, two qualities they must have, in addition to a sound knowledge of the group's business. One is creativeness and originality of mind, the ability to have ideas of their own that are not just copies of other people. In selecting people it is less important whether these are in fact good ideas, so long as they are original. The second quality is judgment: the ability to weed out the good ideas from the bad; this develops later, as a result of learning what works and what doesn't in market terms. Of course a creative leader must have both these qualities, but he also needs the further quality of leadership, the capacity to inspire other creative people, and this is what a member of a group is unlikely to have.

6. *If the creative leader is removed from a group, it becomes an extinct volcano.* As with real volcanoes, it takes time to realize that it has become extinct; but it gradually becomes clear that although it is still efficient, the thing is not bubbling any more. Our society has many extinct volcanoes—societies, magazines, political groups, etc.—which were once exciting and important, and now carry on a staid and routine existence after the glory has departed. The Reform Bill of 1831-1832 created a ferment in English society; but the resulting Reform Club, while still in existence, is not teeming with outrageous modern ideas. An interesting corollary is that if a firm wants to weaken a competitor, one of the cheapest and most effective ways is to identify the creative groups and offer the leaders, or better still the leaders and a couple of their closest colleagues each, lucrative and attractive jobs on its own staff. It is not important

that it should need them itself, although they ought to prove an invaluable addition to the staff; only that the competitor should be deprived of them.

7. *Creative groups define their own projects.* This is not to say they do not need projects given to them—they must have some details of what product is required, how big the budget is, what plant and labor are available, what the time scale is, etc. But the more freedom they are given within those broad limits, the more successful they are likely to be. People tend to devise what they can achieve themselves, and projects devised by creative groups are likely to draw on the skills and expertness and interests that the group possesses. They will not devise a product whose success hinges on metallurgical factors if they have no one with metallurgical qualifications in the group. It therefore follows that there will be more variety in the results of the creative coupling, the bisociation, within the group, if the members of the group have different backgrounds. Of course, if they belong to different species they may not mate at all; but if they all have an almost identical background and experience the intercourse is likely to be incestuous and the offspring eugenically unsound.

I am well aware that listing some of the shared characteristics of creative groups is not the same as providing a formula for starting them. I am equally aware that some of the most important creative ideas have come, without any particular external stimulus, to people working entirely on their own. But great industrial enterprises, although they need the brilliant invention, also need the robust continuing supply of smaller-scale creative ideas harnessed to a productive drive in order to turn the invention into a product. It was in the 1930s that Chester Carlson bisociated his production knowledge of photoconductivity gained as a physicist with his market knowledge of the demand for document copying gained as a patent lawyer to produce the idea of xerography, and he did the experiments privately in his own back kitchen. But it was not until 1960 that Xerox copying started to revolutionize the world's offices and libraries. It was the creative group under Joseph C. Wilson of the Haloid Corporation that transformed a bright idea into a revolution, and made Xerox copying one of the great industrial success stories of a decade. At the moment—such is the speed of advance in science and technology—here may well be a greater number of inventions and discoveries lying around than there are groups capable of exploiting them. There is, after all, no inevitability about the exploitation of inventions: The Byzantines invented clockwork and only used it for levitating the emperor to impress visitors, the Chinese invented gunpowder and used it largely for firework displays, the Tibetans discovered turbine movement and only exploited it for the rotation of prayer wheels. The link between the invention, or the discovery of a principle, and its use to increase the well-being of human beings (whether as users or shareholders) is usually an industrial firm, and within the firm it is the creative group that sees and exploits the possibilities. And if you combine a unique principle like Xerox copying with a creative manufacturing group, you no longer need creative advertising people or creative packaging people or creative public relations people. All you need is a thick order book and a big switchboard.

# 14

## *THE YOGI AND THE COMMISSAR*

If creative groups are the agents of change, the agents of growth, within a state or a corporation, it is not only important to understand how they function and what circumstances give them the best prospect of success; it is also essential to know how to start them. The mechanics of it are fairly straightforward, they are the mechanics of colonization; detaching a group, giving it an objective, an end that has to be achieved, together with resources, the means of achieving it; and thereafter the maximum possible freedom and autonomy in the pursuit of that end. The trouble is, of course, that you may have formed an uncreative group. How can you tell the difference?

The first step in answering that question is to beg it: It is a creative group if it has a creative leader. In fact, you do not create the group, you appoint the leader and let him build it himself. Without him, the group is not a creative group at all, and when he goes it stops being a creative group. It is possible to assign people to him, but it is risky; the group tends to work best if all the key members are chosen by the leader. In the first place, he is the most likely person to know just what kind of person he needs, and in the second place he will probably make a greater effort to weld into the group someone he has selected himself than someone who has been thrust upon him—their success will prove the soundness of his judgment, which is a greater incentive than proving the soundness of someone else's.

The need, therefore, is to understand the nature of the creative leader, to be able to identify him if he is within the organization or recruit him if he is not, and then to create the circumstances in which he can function at his best.

The essence of the creative leader is that he is, in Koestler's phrase, both yogi and commissar. Perhaps the phrase needs explaining, since the concepts it embodies are important to big organizations, which badly need both. Nobody, or virtually nobody, is pure yogi or pure commissar, but most people polarize around one or the other. The yogi is the contemplative individual, the thinker. You will probably find him in the research and development labs, or in the design or planning office. Some of the best and most successful products can be traced back to his original ideas. But he cannot organize or run anything—even his secretary ends up running him. Put him in charge of a department or even a small section and he is a disaster, and what is more he hates it. A common failure of big organizations is to fail to have a separate career and salary ladder for its yogis—to make them run things if they want more status and money. This not only makes them frustrated and dispirited; it also stops them using their best qualities in the service of the corporation, and makes them use their worst ones instead. The commissar, on the other hand, is the man of action. Put him in charge of a sloppy department and he will smarten it up in no time, keep everyone up to the mark, make it work efficiently, and obey his orders on the double. He has never had an idea in his life, and is incapable of questioning the assumption on which his department or the company is running. He gets his ship smart and obedient, rings full ahead, sets the course he has been given on the charts he has been issued, and follows it efficiently and accurately. If there is an iceberg ahead he will run straight into it, because he cannot see beyond the deck rail of his ship or the edges of his chart. Moloch was a commissar.

Good commissars are the backbone of the sort of organization that needs to get a lot of fairly routine work done by a large number of people. Despite the increasing importance of creativeness, they will always be necessary to keep profitable operations running smoothly and efficiently. Their great quality is that they do not need to be chased or prodded: They have the drive inside them, they enjoy pushing things along, they find satisfaction and fulfillment in rushing around getting things done—and it is the actual doing, not the contemplation of the thing done, that is the source of their pleasure. They are the engines; they can pull a lot of freight cars, or even carry a lot of passengers. All they need is a regular supply of standard fuel—money, status, commendation—to keep them going more or less indefinitely. But the tracks have to be laid down for them, and the points are manipulated by others: They could not possibly work out where to go for themselves. However, once they are given a timetable and a destination you do not have to keep checking on whether they have slowed down or wandered off the edge of the track.

Good yogis and good commissars are not all that common. Obviously, therefore, the person who is a combination of both is rarer still. Nevertheless, it is still vital to understand him, because although the spectacular conjunction of the brilliant original thinker with the vigorous and decisive man of action may not crop up more than once in a generation, some sort of combination of the two, in a lesser degree, may well be present in a number of people in a corporation without being fully recognized; or it may have been present in them when they were younger and one or other quality have atrophied since for want of encouragement and opportunity. And these are the people who can lead the creative groups, by virtue of the dual insight that the combination of these qualities gives them.

The importance of this dual insight arises from the difficulty that yogis and commissars have in talking to each other: On any given project they need to be connected up. The trouble is that yogis need to be led by people whom they respect as yogis, and commissars need equally strong commissars to control them. The person who combines the two is the one who makes the connection: He gives effect to the yogi's ideas in such a way that the commissar can turn them into products. In fact, of course, he does much more than this. Because he is part-yogi himself, he understands how the yogis think and work. He knows the sort of ideas you can ask them to have and the sort you cannot. He knows the conditions and circumstances that are conducive to the production of ideas, and the sort that are inhibiting. He knows when they are genuinely stuck and when they are just slacking off. After all, you cannot compel people to produce good ideas. You can compel their presence in certain places at certain times, you can compel the ordinary sort of functions for which they are qualified, but you cannot compel originality and creativeness. They need to be encouraged, stimulated, inspired, and the uncreative mind simply cannot stimulate the creative mind in this way; creative intercourse does not take place.

And, of course, he has the same sort of insight into the commissar. He knows how much he can ask of him, he knows the sort of restraints and restrictions that are irksome and the sort that are welcome, he knows when to advise and when to leave alone. And, as with the yogi, he does not know it through reading and advice, he actually feels it inside himself. If he does not correct a commissar in front of his subordinates, it is not because he has been told

not to but because others have done it to him in the past
and he has hated it. In his creative group there will be some
who are more yogi than commissar, some who are more
commissar than yogi; clearly it is excellent if he is better
than all of them in both areas, but it is not essential. As long
as he is good enough to be respected by the yogis as a yogi
and by the commissars as a commissar, as long as he is
much more of a yogi than any of the commissars and much
more of a commissar than any of the yogis, that is what
matters, because he will have the one thing that none of the
rest possess, namely, an understanding of the whole operation, and not merely sections or aspects of it.

Such people are rare within great corporations. But
why? Is it because so few people with that combination of
qualities are born? Or are they around, but reluctant to join
great corporations? Or are they there inside the corporations but with their qualities atrophying because there is
not the proper scope, the proper structure, for using them
as they should be used? Obviously these questions are
unanswerable, and yet I think there are more people born
with these qualities than using them, because there was a
time when these people were far more common than they
seem to be now. That was a hundred years ago or more,
and the name we give to them is entrepreneur.

The entrepreneur had the dual insight. He understood
how products were designed and made, and he knew how
to organize their production and sale. He was the sort of
individual who made the industrial revolution. After all,
France was at least as scientifically and technologically
advanced as England. The French were the intellectual
leaders of Europe, and yet it was in England that the
revolution happened first. It was a Frenchman, Trésaguet,
who devised the principle for improving roads, but it was
applied much more by MacAdam in England than anyone

in France. It was a Frenchman, Leblanc, who found a way of making soda from salt by treating it with sulfuric acid, but is was on Tyneside that soda was produced in quantities in this way for the soap and glass and textile industries. It was a Frenchman, Berthollet, who in 1785 perfected the idea of chemical bleaching, but it was Tennant in Britain in 1799 who first made a profitable commercial proposition out of it. It was a German who in the seventeenth century invented a process for making sulfuric acid by mixing sulfur and niter with water, but it was Dr. John Wood who went into business with it and brought the price down substantially; and it was John Roebuck who improved the process still further, by using glass instead of lead for containers, and brought the price down from two shillings a ton to twopence halfpenny.

It was these entrepreneurs of the late eighteenth and nineteenth century who seized a scientific revolution and turned it into an industrial revolution. They were the bees in the garden, the yeast in the beer, the detonator in the bomb. The companies they built were not always very secure or very durable, but they formed the thousands of small baronies that have now been conquered by, or merged with, the great modern corporation-kingdoms. An enterprise, to them, was something small, insecure, and perhaps temporary: now it is something vast and permanent. And yet there is still a tendency to think of it as a single enterprise, with room for only one entrepreneur, rather than as an environment in which a number of entrepreneurs can flourish. "In most successful companies, entrepreneurship has disappeared," says the president of the Anglo-Newfoundland Development Company, with some satisfaction.[1] But I suspect what has disappeared is the old-fashioned form of capital raising, risk taking entrepreneurship. The nature of the men remains, but in most companies the opportunities for them have gone.

Perhaps the one organizational factor that most inhibits the evolution of modern entrepreneurs is the cleft between design and production and sales. The essence of the entrepreneur, or the creative leader, is his ability to create a fusion, a synthesis, of all three; he has this intuitive feeling for what people would buy (the sensitive consumer in himself), which belongs to sales, he has the yogi's insight into the creative side, what the designer could be coaxed into designing, and he has the commissar's understanding of how to produce it to the budget and within the time schedule. But these great clefts that exist in so many corporations demand that almost all the people in the firm have either marketing ideas, or production ideas, or design ideas, but never a whole, total idea. By the time you get high enough for all these functions to meet in one person, you have usually reached the chief executive; and he is far too busy to have all the creative ideas in the firm, as well as being too busy to lead all the groups working on them, even if he could think of them.

And yet, if you go back to the early days of the industrial revolution, it is precisely that combination of market sense, production sense, and creative ideas that was the agent of growth. You see it most clearly in the new successful men, not the gentry but the rising parvenu industrialists, the manufacturers, the men of the towns. Since they worked in business and trade, they were not socially acceptable; they were usually dissenters in religion, and so had been cut off from the universities and great public schools. Instead they went to the dissenting academies and studied not Latin and Greek but history and science and mathematics—an unheard-of curriculum for a gentleman. They emerged with lively, independent minds and a restless curiosity about the way things worked. Being a minority in all sorts of ways—religiously and socially, and also financially in that they were rather well off for people who were not gentlemen—they were forced together.

Often they formed societies, and the most famous was the Lunar Society in Birmingham. It met from 1770 onward once a month on Monday nearest to the full moon for intellectual and social discussion. It was an intellectual proving ground: New ideas, especially scientific and technological ideas, were exchanged and discussed all the time, but here it was among practical men with hard business heads, who knew how much things cost to produce, how to produce them, and what they would fetch. Wedgwood belonged to the Lunar Society: so did Erasmus Darwin, the poet and naturalist; so did Boulton, the manufacturer, and his partner Wall, the inventor; Keir, the chemist, and Withering, the medical innovator. James Watt visited them. As an associate they had Benjamin Franklin, who experimented with electricity as well as being a founder of the United States.

And, of course, the group fired off ideas like a machine gun, Wedgwood argued with Watt about heat and then made a new kind of ceramic thermometer work in his pottery ovens. After a discussion on metal alloys, Keir went off and produced a rustless bolt for his friends' factories. Watt invented a copying press in answer to a Lunar Society challenge; it was there that he worked out his steam engine and made it a commercial proposition. Time after time it was the single man who added his knowledge of what the market wanted to his knowledge of new discoveries in science and technology, and then used his entrepreneur's drive to get it made and sold, who gave a fresh forward shove to the developing industrial revolution.

Has the breed died out? Is the mold broken? I find that hard to believe. I would more easily believe that they still exist but have smaller ideas within their own departments, production ideas or marketing ideas for a product that has already been designed, design ideas that are turned down by marketing or modified out of recognition by production development; or else that they find the atmosphere of the great corporations stifling and oppressive, and go off to start management consultancies or advertising agencies or small software houses, or manage pop groups, or go into any area where they can use the gifts they possess on the sort of capital they can raise. I would, in fact, more easily believe that they are still around but that the great corporations do not want them. Or do not deserve them.

# 15

## *THE VISION*

The special understanding of the whole enterprise which distinguishes the creative leader, the yogi-commissar, may of course be wrong; it may be based on insufficient facts or wrongly interpreted evidence or simple miscalculation. Even if it is right, it may not be very important or very lasting. But every now and then, one of these creative leaders hits the jackpot, and the result can be a great organization with a name known all over the world; and the start, or the sudden rise, of many great corporations can be traced back to one man—the founder, the boss, the "old man"—and his flash of insight, his moment of vision. The actual plans may have taken years to work out and implement, there may have been all sorts of additions and modifications, but very often the "old man" himself could put his finger on the point in time where the idea came to him.

Vision is perhaps a rather highly charged word for what could equally be described as simply a good commercial idea, but it does describe both the flash of insight and the enduring principle that may continue to guide the founder for the rest of his life, and perhaps his successors as well. H.J. Heinz founded a business empire on the simple belief that ordinary shoppers on Main Street would pay more for the extra convenience of having food always available in tins, and that he could offer it to them at a price they would pay. Even after his death this simple belief remained the cornerstone of the H.J. Heinz operation. On top of it there is a considerable edifice of theory and practice; what sorts of foods are suitable for this kind of retailing? What kind of advertising—if any? What principles should guide the selection of staff, the choice of suppliers, the level of profit taken, the buying pattern? What number of products would be too many? Too few? Should they start factories in South America? Africa? The questions go on and on, the answers are fashioned by the hammer of logic on the anvil of experience, and over the years a large body of doctrine is built up. But at the root of it there is one man and one vision.

Heinz built one of the few great homogeneous, organic growth empires. Joe Hyman of the British Viyella Textile Federation had a different kind of vision: he looked at a fragmented, inefficient, demoralized cotton industry, with lots of small family firms using capital unproductively, machinery unscientifically, and labor inefficiently, letting sentiment and tradition overrule logic and arithmetic, and scarcely keeping their heads above water. And he had a vision of a new, unified, integrated all-textile industry, reorganized to meet the new and growing markets, dropping the many small unprofitable customers and courting the few large profitable ones, closing unprofitable offices and selling unnecessary freeholds, and using capital intensively in areas like plant and machinery, where it brought in the best return. The result was the Viyella International Federation, which in ten years grew to more than eight times its original size and transformed half of England's cotton industry. Again, he had the creative vision and the qualities of leadership to achieve it.

The classic case of this kind of rationalizing and unifying vision, and the model for all who aim at building an industrial empire from mergers and takeovers, was Bismarck. He looked at a fragmented and inefficient confederation of German states, some independent or semi-independent, some in the Austrian Empire, many of them small and backward; and he saw a single German nation, with all the German-speaking people outside Austria itself unified under the leadership of Prussia. It was by no means as obvious as it may seem in retrospect—they might have been unified under Austria, or have formed an independent confederation that worked for a change. A single German Empire was not a new aspiration, but Bismarck did more than aspire. He saw how it could be done.

Bismarck is so famous as a commissar that the yogi in him is often overlooked. But, in fact, he spent the years from the age of twenty-four to thirty-two as a small landowner, reading a great deal, corresponding a great deal, traveling from time to time, but taking little part in public life. He had previously tried to be a civil servant, but proved to be another of those young men who quickly leave big organizations with considerable relief on both sides. After those contemplative years, he had the ideal bisociative training: first of all learning about the production resources and problems, and then studying the various markets. He studied production during his years in domestic German politics, as a member of the Prussian Diet and delegate to the Frankfurt Parliament. For eleven years he argued and debated and voted, and also observed and noted the strengths and weaknesses of his fellow Germans, what roused them and what angered them, what they would tolerate and what they would resist. Then he moved from production to sales, so to speak; in the next three years he toured the markets; he was ambassador to Russia and France, and went on a mission to Austria and a visit to England. The result was that when he became chief executive, he had the necessary insight into the strengths and weaknesses, the hopes and fears, of both Germany and the other powers. Within nine years, the small Prussian state had become the great German nation.

From the beginning, Bismarck had in mind not only the ultimate shape and size of his own organization, but also its share of the market, namely, the new balance of power in Europe. This meant preventing any merger or agreement between his two chief rivals, France and Russia, and so he tried his best to keep in with Russia to prevent it. Ultimately they united with other rivals to beat the German Empire, but by 1914 Bismarck had been dead for sixteen years, and an inferior management group was in charge.

Bismarck's vision of Prussia came to pass, and yet it resulted in disaster after his death. Why? Was there something inherent in it that was bound to produce disaster in the end? Or was it that those who followed him did not share his vision, did not understand the priorities and emphases, so that they regarded as merely unfortunate or inconvenient events (like the Franco-Russian entente) that Bismarck would have regarded as catastrophic? Obviously this is a question for the historians; and yet there does seem to be an important aspect of leadership in which Bismarck failed, and that is the communication of the vision.

It is rare enough to find someone who combines this vision with the ability to carry it out. And yet if the enterprise is to survive his departure he must do more: He must transmit it. He must be like a powerful transmitter sending out a strong carrier wave for his followers, his staff, his management to tune in to. It is not an accident that this sort of creative leader is often emphatic, voluble, and violent both in condemnation and congratulation; the number of kilowatts he radiates, so to speak, is related to the clarity with which his signal will be received and the distance it will travel. Of course he may only be transmitting prohibitions and orders; even if he is not, it will probably seem that he is to remoter managers who only receive the message after retransmission through a number of relay stations. Nevertheless, if the organization is to endure and progress after his departure, he must communicate his full vision and understanding to the largest possible number of people within the organization.

This sort of communication is, of course, an aspect of good centralization, of getting people tuned into the signal, getting them educated and indoctrinated in the fundamental realities, in the boss's vision. One of the easiest ways to tell if it is there or not is in the matter of economy drives. The mere fact of having to have an economy drive as opposed to constant care and watchfulness is usually evidence of bungling; nevertheless, there are sometimes unforeseeable crises that necessitate an urgent and dramatic cut in expenditure. A bad economy drive usually starts with a message to cut expenditure by 10 percent being passed down the line, until it finally takes effect in the form of cheaper carbon paper, lower-quality pencils, postponement of redecoration and refurnishing, and a number of even more trivial token gestures that make it possible to say, "Well, we've economized up to the hilt, we can't save a penny more." By contrast, a good economy drive comes from the very top; it is an aspect of the vision. The boss conceives in his own mind how the whole organization can best survive and prosper on 10 percent less expenditure. It may mean putting off a major expansion, cutting out a complete department or product or service, or rethinking the way the whole enterprise will have to move over the coming years.

One of the most spectacular examples of this sort of economy was carried out at the British Admiralty by

Admiral Sir John "Jackie" Fisher, who was first sea lord from 1904 to 1910 (and also 1914-1915), and one of the most unmistakable examples of the creative leader. Year after year he cut the naval estimates dramatically while steadily increasing the efficiency and fighting power of the British fleet.[1] He was able to do this by means of his own creative vision of the navy, which was very different from the navy he found on his appointment. He imposed an overriding priority, namely, so organizing it that it could defeat the German fleet. The maintenance of half a dozen frigates for social purposes in every port from Mombasa to Hong Kong immediately became a questionable luxury, whereas the building of dreadnoughts, all-big-gun battleships with much greater speed and armor and firepower than the old ones, went to the top of the list. In the face of Fisher's passionate and violent assertion of priorities, luxury expenditure (in his terms) fell away. Before very long the Admiralty staff had tuned in to this deafening signal, and could share Fisher's vision of a lean, muscular fighting navy concentrated in a few key stations, instead of a vast obsolescent prestige force scattered about all over the seven seas for ancient historical or traditional reasons. Despite laying down more and more dreadnoughts, the navy estimates dropped year by year. Economy does not need an actuary, it needs a visionary.

Trivial and niggardly economy drives are one aspect of absence of vision, or failure to transmit it. Another is frequent requests for "rulings": There are constant requests for "rulings" on all sorts of points where it should not be necessary; and the further up they have to go the more weakly the signal is being transmitted—if indeed there is a message to transmit. It is the sort of firm where lower-line managers take (or do not take) actions and decisions that horrify the top management, and that spring not from ineptitude but simply from not realizing what the firm is about; like the firm that had to keep its most precious and sensitive customer waiting an hour for a presentation of the product they were trying to sell him, for a value of nearly half a million dollars, because the workmen were still putting up ceiling tiles in the projection theater. It could have been finished the night before, but the house manager was not allowed to authorize overtime over fifteen dollars without advance written approval, and this would have cost over twenty-four dollars, so he had to put it off to the next morning. Oh, yes, they knew there were some bigwigs or other coming along, but there was nothing he could do about it.

But worst of all, the firm is liable to creeping paralysis of the initiative. The great advantage of a strong and clear signal from the top is that even quiet junior managers, when they are tuned into it, can make good independent decisions without worrying. They can answer telephone queries, even press queries, sensibly and decisively rather than timidly and evasively, because they know what the business is about. It is always the court of last instance which the executive has in mind. If this finally comes up before the board, will they agree that I did the right thing?

If he understands the business, if he is fully tuned in, he will almost always know the answer. If not, he will hardly ever know and therefore be as cautious and indecisive as possible. This same sort of knowledge also operates in another dimension; it gives the executive the security of knowing his place in the pecking order. One of the most common unspoken questions in executives' minds at times of dispute is, "If I go in front of the boss and say 'either X goes or I go,' who goes?" The more clearly every executive knows the answer for any given value of X, the greater his sense of security. If he thinks the answer is wrong, he may quit, but he may be right to go, and it may be in the long-term interest of the firm that he should. In all these cases it is not the intermediate managers who signify; what counts is the likely judgment of the supreme court. It counts not because the case will ever reach it, but because if the signal is transmitted strongly enough the case will be settled long before it ever gets there, since everyone knows what the verdict will be. This is one of the most common reasons why young executives question policy decisions and rulings; not because they necessarily disagree with them, but because they are trying to tune in to the carrier wave, to understand the thinking behind it all. A ruling from the top is a manifestation of this central vision (or indeed lack of it), but it may need interpreting to novices, and a question like "Why aren't we going for the top bracket of the market?" or "Why are we doing this job on batch instead of on production line?" for all its apparently critical implications, is really only a search for a clearer understanding. It is by answering this sort of question properly and fully, and going on with the discussion provoked by the answer, that the vision from the top can be spread throughout the firm: in fact, by dialogue. Equally, the vision, the understanding, can be blocked by the answer, "Because I say so. Now shut up and get on with it."

It may, of course, be that even at the top there is no vision, and that the decision is just a bad decision. In which case "Shut up and get on with it," while never a good answer, is probably the best available.

# 16

## *FAME AND FEEDBACK*

It is strange that Shakespeare, who had such profound insight into so many corners of the human heart, should never have understood the nature of the leader. He reveals this lack of understanding in several different ways, but in none so clearly as the speech he puts into the mouth of Henry V on the eve of Agincourt. The essence of it is the unwelcome burden of responsibility that kingship carries with it, the "hard condition, twin-born with greatness" and the unattractiveness and inadequacy of ceremony as compensation. This is typical of the yogi's view of the commissar—he sees all the worry and responsibility of the job and nothing else. It is a perfectly reasonable attitude for a weak, reflective king like Henry VI, but not for a bold and dashing leader like Henry V. But Shakespeare was chiefly yogi, and to him the thought of the time "when all those legs and arms and heads, chopp'd off in battle, shall join together at the latter day, and cry all, 'we died at such a place,'"[1] dominates any other consideration. It is not however the dominating idea to the commissar; Marlowe's *Tamburlaine,* when he exclaims:

> Is it not passing brave to be a King,
> And ride in triumph through Persepolis?[2]

is really expressing the dominant idea to the commissar: the exhilaration of it.

It is still possible to taste something of the exhilaration of kingship today, though not as a constitutional monarch. The president or chairman of a great corporation does not taste it any more. But the entrepreneur, the creative leader, with a small privately owned company, still has something of that independent authority. He is commander-in-chief of the army, directing sales campaigns and deciding on products; he is also prime minister, making the long-term decisions on policy, as well as foreign secretary, conducting the most important negotiations with suppliers and customers; he is head of the civil service, in charge of all the internal organization; and he is lord chief justice, the ultimate court of appeal. Economists note a marked unwillingness on the part of owners of small manufacturing businesses to borrow money for expansion in exchange for a piece of the equity of their company. I suspect it is not lack of ambition, but fear of the real worries of kingship: not total personal responsibility, since that is what they welcome and enjoy; on the contrary, it is the prospect of a share in control and a management team, converting them from autocrats into constitutional monarchs, which makes them hesitate. Power is freedom, and it is not the image of a man shaking off a burden that springs to their mind, as it would to Shakespeare's: it is of a man walking into a prison.

There is a sense, too, in which being a boss is easier than being a manager. The boss has to succeed, to produce results, and so does his manager. But the boss can take what action he likes within the confines of law, union agreements, etc., whereas the manager has superiors, whom he must persuade to create for him conditions in which he can succeed. He needs all the other qualities and diplomacy as well: He must not antagonize his superiors. The boss does not have any superiors: He may have to be polite to customers and prospects, but he is not their subordinate, and one reason for his being a boss—perhaps the most power-ful—is that he is not cut out to be a subordinate.

It is, I suppose, impossible to generalize about the personal qualities and motives of the creative leader, the entrepreneur figure; certainly they differ widely in all sorts of matters like tastes and habits and manners and religious beliefs and so on. And yet a great many of them seem to share a small number of quite precise characteristics, which seem to stem from a powerful ego. The powerful ego in itself is hardly surprising: to build a successful enterprise from small beginnings, whether independently or within a great corporation, demands an obsessive effort. Holi-days, savings, spare-time interests, wives, children, sleep are all sacrificed to the cause of the enterprise. Shakespeare may believe that the driving force is a sense of duty and responsibility, but a driving ego that identifies itself with the success or failure of the enterprise gives a stronger urge. The form it often seems to take is a desire for recognition, a kind of vanity that seems to be an assured arrogance but, in fact, is not hard to wound—although a wound is only a spur to more violent effort. It also seems to go with a mild-to-strong persecution complex, a feeling that those who are not completely won over are enemies united by personal animosity in deadly conspiracy. Both Fisher and Bismarck saw only friends or foes, and it is a phenomenon often spoken of by those who encounter creative leaders; they love and they hate more readily than other people. But it all helps to drive them on to scorn delights and live laborious days. Fame is the spur, according to Milton, and the Romans recognized this when they awarded triumphs to successful generals. A day was set aside as holiday, the streets were lined with crowds, and the victorious general on horseback led his soldiers through the streets of Rome followed by a great train of captives and the spoils of war, up to the triumphal arch dedicated to him forever. The exhausted general, flagging in the Libyan heat or the Dacian rain, only had to close his eyes and see the adulation on the faces of the cheering crowd, the eternal marble monument to his conquests, and he would redouble his efforts, not for Rome but for personal glory. This desire for public acclaim is not nearly so well satisfied in our modern society—a few magazine articles, an appearance on television, or an award from the government are the nearest to a Roman triumph that the modern tycoon can hope for, and they are a long way away.

This combination of egotism, vanity, selfishness, desire for recognition, and speed at taking offense are not, of course, the most engaging characteristics. Some are more aware of them than others, and control them better, but it is rare for them not to be there in some form. And yet these people very often, almost always, collect a devoted group of people around them. One reason for this is their very strong personal magnetism; another is that they provide an objective, a purpose, the task of building something, which most people find attractive and many irresistible. They have their eye on a goal, and somehow those who work for them are given to feel that they are not just earning a salary, but serving a cause. The leaders, to do them justice, usually give loyalty in the same ample measure as they receive it; and yet, by a strange paradox, those who work close to them always feel slightly insecure: They would follow him anywhere, but they always feel he might decide to replace them, and yet they do not resent this. "He for God only, she for God in him"—Milton's expression of the relationship between Adam and Eve is often true of the leader and his group. They follow him, the embodiment of the ideal, but he pursues only his objective. And much as he values his team or groups or followers, they must not come between him and the cause, not slacken in the great task; and because all other pulls—home, leisure, family—are so weak in him by comparison with this task, he assumes they are equally weak in them and seems indifferent to any pleas of wanting time off or needing to get home before dawn. The relationship is indeed often a bit like love in its intensity and demands, and those who once were of the group and then leave are regarded like former mistresses who walked out—passion is dead, but the memory of the intimacy is never completely erased.

Another regular complaint about these leaders is that they meddle too much in details that they should leave to others. Partly this is because they never completely trust anyone; because they are the only one with the complete vision, they can never be quite sure that even the most trusted of lieutenants fully understands the exact relative importance of all considerations. But there is another reason: A complex project can fail on a tiny detail of date or price or quality, and the entrepreneur feels it impossible not to check, since his ego is so completely tied up in the outcome. And the real creative leader does understand the details of the business right down to the roots, he knows how long all important things take and what they cost and what corners he can cut and what risks he takes if he does. At the highest level, he can only deal in millions effectively if he has previously dealt in hundreds of thousands, and tens of thousands, and thousands, before that. A million dollars doesn't mean anything if you come to it fresh, only if you have worked up to it, assimilating the previous stages. As Spenser says,

> How canst thou these greater secrets know
> That dost not know the least thing of them all?
> Ill can he rule the great, that cannot reach the small.[3]

There is no doubt that running a creative group successfully can be heady wine. The great danger point comes
when the leader is tempted to believe his own myth, to
think that perhaps he has got some uncanny gift, that he is
indeed a superman. After all, there is considerable evidence: the success of the enterprise, the routing of rivals,
the obvious admiration of such able, brilliant people; perhaps failure is impossible. It is a tempting draught, but to
drink it deadens the vital nerve, the raw nerve that must
always be kept alive and sensitive, however painful, since
the pain is the warning of greater danger.

This raw nerve is in fact the feedback mechanism, and
it is an aspect of the sensitive, easily wounded ego. The
Molochs, the simple commissars, frequently lack this feedback, which is why they need guidance from above; but the
man at the top cannot do without it. This nerve receives
even very faint signals that everything is not going right.
The others may be perfectly happy, but they are not the
ones who will suffer most if things go wrong, and the man
who will be most hurt by failure is also likely to be the one
who is most wary of it, most alert for warnings. It may only
be a faint intonation in an important customer's voice on
the telephone, a casual snatch of conversation heard in a
shop, a sales figure that ought to have been a shade better:
signs that others would dismiss, if indeed they noticed
them at all. But the creative leader notices and worries and
plans to close the gap, to make the necessary improvement
before it is visible to others.

One of the paradoxes of the leader is that he cannot
succeed without confidence or without doubt. His own
confidence is essential for the morale of the whole group;
in dark moments it is his shining certainty that keeps them
going. And yet he must constantly question and suspect
everything that he is doing, he must be alert for the first

hint of error or failure, he must keep his feedback nerve as raw and sensitive as possible. This also involves listening to criticisms from his subordinates. (The violent autocrat surrounded by obsequious yes-men is a more common figure in fiction than in fact.) Of course, there are leaders who deaden their feedback nerve, because the success is too intoxicating or the messages of failure too many and too painful—Hitler, for example, or Napoleon, or maybe Henry Ford—but it is usually the prelude to a disastrous crash. The British victory in the Battle of Britain has been attributed[4] to the fact that Air Marshal Sir Hugh Dowding and Air Vice Marshal Sir Keith Park proved capable of standing up to Churchill while their German counterparts could not stand up to Goering, which is another way of saying that Churchill was alive to feedback and Goering was not. The successful creative leader is often willing to listen to criticism from anybody from his vice president to the office cleaner, and his subordinates are often infuriated when they discover the lowly source of the complaints that are being forwarded to them.

One of the great difficulties is that the source of the fault may have been in the leader's own decision or idea. How is a man whose vanity, whose ego, is his driving force, to recognize and admit that the blame is his? Marcus Wallenberg, the great creative banker-industrialist behind much of Sweden's industrial success, made a most interesting observation about this. He was chairman of some ten companies and on the board of a further fifty, but in his youth he was an international tennis player. He set great store by reaching the top in competitive sport, on the grounds that to succeed at that level you can no longer explain away defeat by the weather or the state of the court or your opponent's extraordinary luck. You have to analyze your own play quite dispassionately, searching for and analyzing your errors and weaknesses in order to correct them where possible and to plan your future game to conceal the ones you cannot correct. Wallenberg believed that this training early in life taught him one of the most important lessons he had ever learned, the lesson of seeking the cause of failure in yourself. It may be inevitable for a young man to invest his ego in the rightness of his decisions and assessments, the high quality of his own ideas and suggestions, and the infallibility of his judgment of people, but these are dangerous stocks for the leader of the enterprise to hold shares in. There comes a time when he has to sell his holding in them, and reinvest his ego in the overall success of the enterprise and that alone. So long as that prospers, his ego is satisfied; and instead of resisting the thought that he may possibly have made a mistake in the past, his ego gets further satisfaction from his being big enough to admit that he was wrong. It is for this reason that a resounding failure at some early point in his career can be an excellent formative ingredient in a leader's character. The BBC once did a hoax television program on April Fool's Day in which they showed a film of the Italian spaghetti harvest, with the smiling peasant girls gathering great skeins of spaghetti from the branches of the trees. One of the many people who were taken in was the director general of the BBC. I thought it did him great credit. The reason, he explained later, was that for most of his life he had thought that peanuts grew on trees. When he discovered they grew in the ground, he immediately opened his mind to the possibility of his being wrong about other lifelong assumptions that were not verified by observation. It may not have done him much good on this occasion, but the principle is still a sound one.

There is one other factor, in addition to the raw nerve and the need for success and the other qualities of creative leadership, that the successful leader must have: time. The others are inherent in his nature and this is not, but to build something that endures, it is of the greatest importance to have a long tenure of office, to rule for many years. You can achieve quick success in a year or two, but nearly all the great tycoons have continued their building for much longer. Alexander did wonders in eight years, but the empire of his dreams fell to pieces when he died, whereas Augustus in forty-four years transformed Rome from a disintegrating republic into the greatest empire ever known, just as Alfred Sloan in twenty-three years transformed General Motors from a disintegrating assembly of companies into one of the greatest industrial empires yet established. It takes time after all, often several years, for people to see whether your decisions were good or bad; it takes time to put into key posts men chosen by yourself; it takes time to get the confidence and respect of colleagues; it takes time to stop bad old practices before you can start good new ones. Given that time, a mystique starts to grow: You change slowly from a novice among veterans to a veteran among novices. To have a first-rate leader for a long time is very fortunate. To have three first-rate managing directors, each holding the job for a third of a century, can work wonders: It turned a tiny, insignificant emirate in Asia Minor into the Ottoman Empire, which endured for over six hundred years.[5] It was three strong managing directors[6]—despite a brief and bloody interlude—who turned England from an island split and exhausted by warring factions into a united and prospering nation, victors over the Armada, trading and colonizing all over the world. Henry VI's disastrous forty-year reign shows that length of tenure is not enough, but without it none of the other qualities have a chance to come to full flowering.

# 17

## CHAMBER OF HORRORS

"All happy families resemble each other," says Tolstoy at the start of *Anna Karenina*; "each unhappy family is unhappy in its own way." It may also be true that all good leaders resemble each other, while each bad leader is bad in his own way, just as there is only one kind of good health but many kinds of sickness. Nevertheless, there are certain recurring types of bad leaders who are sufficiently common in states and corporations for it to be worth listing some of them, not merely as an awful warning, but also because it is sometimes easier to deduce principles and general laws by seeing what happens when they are violated than when they are kept.

I have already talked (Chapter 16) about the Hitler-Napoleon-Henry Ford type of bad leader, the one who lets his raw nerve become anesthetized. The leader who surrounds himself with yes-men is like a pilot flying blind with instruments that tell him only what they believe he wants to see instead of their true readings. Moreover, that sort of dictator drives all strong, independent, original minds out of the organization and silences all critical discussions of his policies, so that when the crash comes there is usually no alternative policy that anyone has been formulating and no leader of any quality there to take over command. When Henry Ford took over all the decision making of his company and set spies on his managers to try and catch them making decisions on their own, he was ensuring that the crash, when it came, would be cataclysmic; indeed it is believed it was fifteen years before the firm showed a profit again.[1] When people say that absolute dictatorship carries within it the seeds of its own destruction, what they really mean is that it does not carry within it the seeds of its own survival.

Ford's, however, is a special kind of bad leadership, since you have to graduate to it through considerable and continued success. The kind of bad leaders who populate this chamber of horrors never climb high enough for such a reverberating fall; their career is a succession of tumbles into the holes they have dug for themselves.

## King Lear

Of all the fallacies about leadership, the one about *King Lear* seems to be the most attractive. It is so neat; you remain the chief executive, but you delegate complete authority to two or three divisional managers. They have the worry and the sweat, and you keep the honor and the glory. The trouble comes, of course, as Lear discovered, when the divisional managers—in his case Goneril and Regan, with the dukes of Albany and Cornwall—start to turn nasty. In his case they refused him all information about their activities (turned him out of their castles), they took away his few remaining powers and staff (dismissed his bodyguard), and left him desolate, powerless, and howling piteously about ingratitude. It is another instance of Shakespeare's lack of insight into leadership that, while he does not ask us to admire Lear, he expects us to be shocked and horrified by the unnatural behavior of his daughters and their consorts. It is reasonable to be horrified, but not shocked or surprised, and whatever else their behavior may be, it is certainly not unnatural in power and leadership terms, even though one may hope that most families get on better than the Lears. Lear was asking for it. Worry and responsibility are part of the price of power. Real power does not lie in documents and memos outlining your terms of reference and area of jurisdiction: it lies in what you can achieve in practice. The boss's secretary can wield great power, like the king's mistress, without any authority at all—or at least not the sort you can show anybody. Equally, the head of a big division or company can be powerless, just as Lear was powerless, despite any number of theoretical powers. Power lies in the acceptance of your authority by others, their knowledge that if they try to resist you they will fail and you will succeed. And so the boss who does a Lear is liable to discover that Goneril and Regan, the production director and the marketing director, ignore his directives: and he realizes that the only statutory power he has left is to fire them. But it is made clear to him that if he does fire them, each has a better job waiting with an expanding competitor, and has arranged to take the twelve key people of his division with him. If the Lear has to report to a board, that is that: His power has vanished. But even if he owns privately 100 percent of the equity, he is still ditched. All he can do is accept defeat or do a Samson and destroy the firm; and while Samson makes a great tragic hero, he would have been an appalling managing director.

Comfortable leadership is a contradiction in terms. The leader must make sure everyone knows that the toughest decisions are his responsibility, that however great their worries they can in the last resort pass them to him, whereas he cannot pass them to anyone. They pay him for that with a part of their freedom, their independence, their autonomy—a sort of authority tax that he exacts and they

pay with a willingness that is in proportion to their satisfaction with the use he puts it to. As long as they see he is
using that authority of theirs to fight an important battle or
carry out useful reforms, they go on paying, but when they
see it wasted or frittered away, and also find they can get
away without paying it, then they stop. If they realize that
they are now taking the toughest decisions on their own,
they realize, as Goneril and Regan realized, that they are
of greater value to the enterprise than he is. There is a
simple equation:

$$\text{authority} + \text{responsibility} = \text{power}$$
$$\text{authority} - \text{responsibility} = \text{deposition}$$

The Roman Emperor Augustus, who was the exact opposite of Lear in that he wanted the reality of power without
the appearance, took care to preserve personal command
of the most troublesome provinces. It may have been that
he was not quite sure that anyone else could handle them;
but it may have been that he knew that if he delegated to
someone else the responsibility for the toughest job in the
empire, and authority over the biggest army in the empire,
he might be creating an even greater problem than he was
solving.

## Coeur de Lion

Richard Coeur de Lion was one of those managers who was
first rate at his own job but never grew up into the wider
responsibilities of managing the whole business. He was a
marvelous soldier, but when he became king he could not
give up soldiering. He went off to the crusades, which at
that time had a fairly low priority, and left England to get
into deeper and deeper trouble. Moreover, the capital appropriations he made to the crusades were ridiculously

high and desperately needed for other parts of the enterprise. He was a great warrior hero, but a disastrous king. There are many Coeur de Lions in industry. They are the ones who cannot let go, like the sales managers who cannot make the transition to management. They still go out and sell to all the big customers themselves, instead of creating a context and formulating a policy within which others can sell more effectively. If they become chief executive, their professional craft-pride blinds them to the real faults in the organization—they just think it is because the salesmen are not as good as they were in the old days. It is, after all, a difficult transition from skilled production engineer or process planner to production manager, from salesman to sales director: It means abandoning the craft skill on which all your security and self-esteem and reputation have rested, or at least reducing its importance compared to the unknown demands of managing others who possess them. The higher that skill, the harder it is to abandon. The sign of a potential manager in a craftsman, in fact, is not craft excellence; it is the willingness to see his craft as only part of the whole problem, and not to blame other departments for what is beyond their control. As a production man he may justly blame sales for faulty estimating or insufficient information at the design stage, but not for wanting things in a hurry if the competitive situation clearly demands it. But the budding Coeur de Lion will not see it that way: Wisdom and folly in others are judged only by the criterion of how easy or difficult they make his job.

## Nicholas II

Just as the good leader picks out the one piece of disturbing news from a mass of encouraging reports, so there is a kind of leader who manages to see only the tiny crumbs of comfort and ignores and shuts himself off from all the signs of approaching disaster. Nicholas II, with the assistance of his wife, managed to build himself a fantasy world that he inhabited up to 1917. You would have thought the signs were unmistakable, but he managed to mistake them and reassure himself with trivia. There seems to be a wonderful power of self-deception latent in humankind, and adversity brings it to the surface in weak leaders. They pick on one or two good statistics, a reported flattering remark by a customer about the product, a tiny setback suffered by a rival firm, and shut all the rest out of their mind. There always seem to be people willing to pander to this, to provide false or misleading encouragement, even while the mob is at the gates of the Winter Palace. The people who see what is coming and issue warnings become terrible bores, and the fairyland courtiers all giggle about them after they have left the meeting. This sort of weak leader is usually a believer in the philosopher's stone, some simple remedy for all the ills. "Our image is wrong, that's all." "It's just that we have this communications problem." Just as Nicholas, and more especially his tsarina, fell for Rasputin, so his organizational counterparts become attached to other charlatans who offer specious panaceas. It may be a public relations adviser, a management consultant, or just some strange *éminence grise* they met at a party. The mystic remedy may be a new organization chart, a computer, a prestige advertising campaign, or any other form of occult practice that cannot be proved to have succeeded or failed until it is too late to remember exactly what was claimed for it. It may even be something quite sensible. But as long as Nicholas is there, it will not have a chance.

# George I

Although he was king of England, in his heart George I (like George II) remained first and foremost the Elector of Hanover. He spent much of his reign there, for all its comparative insignificance. As a result, his managers started to get control of the firm—the Cabinet took over more and more of the king's power. It is a defect similar to Richard I's—in his case the boss who takes over after being chief executive of one of the subsidiary divisions or companies, but cannot outgrow it. He still spends a disproportionate amount of time there, lets its affairs occupy his thoughts far more than they should, and only seems really happy when he is back there with his old colleagues.

# George III

It is always unfortunate for a new boss to meet a lot of hostility soon after his appointment, but George III found the wrong way out of trouble. Instead of calmly distinguishing between what was sensible and what was just claptrap in the opposition arguments, he pigheadedly shut his ears to the whole of them and governed through docile, subservient ministers who either shared his political deafness or, for the sake of private advantage, were prepared to feign it. You do not have to work long in an organization governed in this way to understand the fury and ridicule and contempt it arouses in those who are ignored and excluded—especially when events prove them right. Few chief executives who do this can achieve anything quite as spectacular as the loss of America in consequence, but there are usually plenty of smaller disasters open to them.

# Edward the Confessor

Disaster seems almost inevitable for the philosopher-king who is all philosopher and no king. The disaster Edward contrived did not strike until after he died in 1066: He left the government of England in the hands of Harold Godwinson during his reign, but nominated William of Normandy to succeed to the throne after his death; Edward was a saintly man, much given to retirement, contemplation, and prayer, and hence the Battle of Hastings. Henry VI was another saintly figure; he let England in for the Wars of the Roses. The thoughtful, intellectual chief executive who is much happier on his lecture tour or writing his book or chairing royal commissions and government committees and addressing groups of dons and civil servants than in the tough, messy, worrying business of running the organization is likely to say that "the organization runs itself." The truth is that someone else is running it, at best, or (in descending order of desirability) two, three, four, or five different people are all competing to run it for him, until it finally becomes like a bus with half the passengers trying to drive and the rest trying to collect the fare. It is clear from *The Tempest* that Prospero was an Edward the Confessor:

> The government I cast upon my brother,
> And to my state grew stranger, being transported
> And rapt in secret studies...

He retired to his library, left all the authority and responsibility to Antonio, but expected to remain undisputed Duke of Milan. When his brother deposed him, he looked pained and astonished, whereas quite clearly he had it coming to him. Frank Pace of General Dynamics (see Chapter 5) seems to have been an Edward the Confessor, a yogi in commissar's clothing; a trained lawyer who had held distinguished yogi jobs like Director of the Budget and Secretary of the Army, but had never run a business till he took over General Dynamics with its 106,000 employees and nine feudal baronies.

## Pussycat

One of the few memorable sermons of my schooldays was preached on the text:

> "Pussycat, pussycat, where have you been?"
> "I've been to London to see the Queen."
> "Pussycat, pussycat, what did you there?"
> "I saw a little mouse under a chair."

The preacher's question was, "Why had the cat not seen the queen?" It might be, of course, that the queen was not there. But it might be that the queen was there all the time, sitting on the chair, but the cat, being only a cat, saw nothing except the mouse. After all, if you are only a cat, your eyes are not looking at where the queen might be, and in any event, your mind is not capable of comprehending anything so great and splendid even if your eyes were to see it. I will not labor the theological point, but there are also pussycat executives. They do not see the great problem, only the little ones. You can judge a leader by the size of problem he tackles—people nearly always pick a problem their own size, and ignore or leave to others the bigger or smaller ones. The chief executive should be thinking about the long-term changes that will bring growth or decay to different parts of the enterprise, not fussing over day-to-day problems: Other people can cope with the waves, it's his job to watch the tide. And yet you find boards of directors spending hours discussing priorities in the allocation of parking space when they move into the new building, you find executives deliberately holding a meeting down to trivial points, because that is all they can cope with. The trouble is that if the top management is thinking at too low a level, there are no levels left for the rest of the staff to think at, and this spawns a generation of managerial pygmies.

This is, unfortunately, by no means a complete list of the types of bad managers or the roads to ruin. If it is to be more than a chamber of horrors or a handy recognition chart, there ought to be some positive guiding principles to be deduced from it.

Looking back over the list, they seem to be:

1. Always take the heaviest responsibility yourself.

2. Your own craft skill is not a rampart for your defense but a barrier to your advance.

3. Always hunt for the disquieting evidence.

4. Spend most of your time among the most powerful group in the organization.

5. Win opposition over to your side or at least to neutrality; don't raise your own private army to fight it.

6. Remember that thought is a prelude, and not an alternative, to action.

7. Look for problems through a telescope, not through a microscope.

# 18

## BARONS AND COURTIERS

The more common term is "line and staff," but barons and courtiers better describes their natures, and their separate relationships with the king, the chief executive. It is not only the fundamental division within an organization, it also reflects a difference between two types of manager, two types of nature. You see it in the army, where the general has his staff officers—operations, planning, intelligence, etc., on the one hand, and his corps commanders on the other. You see it in the corporation, where the chief executive has his personnel manager, training manager, publicity manager, finance manager, company secretary, legal adviser, etc., on the one hand, and his divisional managers or product managers or regional managers on the other. It is the same as the king with his chamberlain and steward and chancellor and treasurer and justiciar on one hand, and his barons or provincial governors on the other. Their functional division is between thought and action: Some things have to be done, other things have to be planned and organized and recorded. Their personal division is between yogi and commissar: The staff courtiers polarize round the yogi type, the line barons round the commissar type, although at the highest level each probably has a fair element of the other in his makeup.

The situation is always liable to be tense. Lord Wavell has pointed out[1] that Hotspur's speech about the prisoners[2] is a perfect expression of the line's resentment of staff, which is as old as war itself. The medieval baron, busy keeping invaders from the borders of the realm, doubtless felt the same emotion when at the height of the trouble he heard of some new land tax that would take all the hard-built morale out of his peasant-soldiers when they heard about it. And the same goes for the regional manager, short of salesmen in a tough competitive situation when he gets a document from head office demanding six pages of statistical returns, notifying him of a new invoicing procedure, and telling him to cut back on expense claims and use of company cars by his salesmen. The baron thinks the courtiers are remote, airy-fairy smartalecks who ought to spend a few weeks at the sharp end just to learn what it is all really about, the courtier thinks the barons are dim, out-of-date, unsystematic, unimaginative cowboys who cannot see beyond their noses. All too often they can both prove it.

The link between the two of them is the king, the general, the chief executive, and obviously there is a temptation for him to lean too far toward the one or the other. But in practice the temptation is usually much more toward valuing the courtier above the baron than vice versa. After all, the courtier is close at hand and the baron is usually far away. The courtier has the king's ear far more often, and can observe him closely to find out which people and what ideas are in favor or out of favor and can angle suggestions and requests so as to cash in on the current mood. In the corporation they know that "coordinate," "rationalize," and "uncluttered," are the current in-words, and that "streamline," "image," and "formula" have been rather overdone and are best left alone for a while, whereas the poor old regional manager is still behind the times, out of touch with the court fashions, and puts all the wrong words in his memorandum. Courtiers always seem to have time to write lengthy and persuasive papers to promote their pet schemes, while the barons say they're too damned busy to put it on paper and what's the telephone for anyway? Courtiers are good at flattery, barons take pride in being bad at it.

The rise of the courtier coincides with the subjugation of the baron; they are part of the king's armory in his struggle to dominate rebellious lords, part of the mechanism for converting a feudal system into a corporate state. And yet, in the end, it is the barons who matter and not the courtiers; and the king who listens more to his courtiers than his barons, and values them more highly, is heading for trouble. A baron is a leader like the king; a smaller-scale version, perhaps, but he needs all the same qualities even if not quite to the same degree. The baron's success is real, unarguable, objective; anyone can see it. Either he keeps order in his lands, keeps the marauders out, and collects all his taxes, or he does not. Either he fulfills his production quota within his budget and up to standard, or he does not. But who is to say if a courtier has succeeded or failed? How do you set a quota for the public relations officer? Or the personnel manager? The firm may have an appalling press reputation and a disastrously high staff turnover, but you just try pinning that on the courtier responsible. He can prove conclusively that it has happened despite all his vigilance and effort, and that without his brilliance, his imagination, and his unflagging labors the situation would be far worse. His success or failure is not objective like the baron's, it is in the eye of the beholder. He is as successful as the chief executive believes he is. For this reason, his standing at court becomes all-important to him; he is one of those wretched men who hang on princes' favors. He is not a king himself on a small scale, like the baron, he is an extension of a particular aspect of kingship: public relations, training, personnel policy, finance, and administration are all proper concerns of the chief executive, and if he appoints someone to look after them for him, that person is a sort of secretary rather than a sort of leader. Unlike the baron, he has no following, no sphere of power. Beaverbrook in his struggle with Bevin during World War II lamented that he was only a court favorite. He drew his power only from Churchill's authority, and if Churchill took away his authority and his protecting hand, Beaverbrook was powerless. But Bevin was a baron; Bevin took the labor force of the nation with him if he walked out. His power was visible, objective, and formidable, and Churchill could only resist it at his peril, whereas he could drop Beaverbrook whenever he chose.

Leadership demands a constant balancing of priorities, at whatever level; but the courtier's job is to think of the part rather than the whole. The chief executive has to decide between the competing claims on the company purse of, say, a raise for the managerial staff, an increased advertising appropriation, a new office block, a higher dividend, and a number of other desirable forms of expenditure; and so, at lower levels, do all the barons. But the courtier thinks of getting the maximum for his own department, not only for the good he believes he can do with it, but also as proof to others of his skill and success and standing.

Quite often a strong creative leader will need a number of people to sweep up after him, to make up for his shortcomings. He may well be impatient of orderly routine procedures, and need a courtier who can follow around and impose some sort of system on his innovations so that less-gifted people can carry them out efficiently. He may be terse and brusque, and need another courtier who can handle people diplomatically and smooth ruffled feelings, and say the right things to the press and the government. He may be too preoccupied with the task in hand to think of the general welfare of the staff, and another courtier may be essential to supply considerateness and humanity to the enterprise. But all these people have it in them to destroy the corporation, because of each courtier's imbalance. If the leader goes and one of them takes over, it can be disastrous, because if they were temperamentally right for their other job, their temperament is unlikely to be right for the top job. Excessive preoccupation with press comment and the public image, at the expense of long-term objectives, can be extremely dangerous. So can excessive preoccupation with welfare and "everyone getting along with each other"; so can excessive preoccupation with administrative and financial tidiness. All are important, but they should come after policy has been formed, to test and perhaps modify it; they should not be an important ingredient in its formation.

The introduction of change probably gives the greatest stimulus to the hostility between barons and courtiers. The baron instantly expects that the courtier is imposing a load of extra work on him simply out of his own laziness or to further some pet private scheme. The merit of the change has to be blindingly obvious to win acceptance, and if it is not, the natural baronial reaction is to say it will not work. And since it is he who will have to make it work, it is easy for him to prove he was right. The courtier, of course, will not believe the baron and will put his objections down to narrowmindedness or obstinacy or both. Equally, if the baron wants change, the courtier is liable to put it down to his shifting the blame for failure off the operator and onto the system. If the regional sales manager says that salesmen are being sent to him with inadequate qualifications and the wrong training, and that the posts are wrongly structured, this will mean a lot of work for the courtiers responsible for recruitment and training and personnel policy if he is right. Much better to put it down to his preparing his excuse for not reaching his forecast. But the odds are with the baron, because he is in touch with the realities in a way the courtier is not. It is infuriating if some field commander tells the War Office that the serried rank of men with muskets does not work on the battlefield any more, that Napoleon is using smaller bands of skirmishers who are playing hell with it, and that what is wanted is a mobile, flexible light division. After all, it means re-equipping the men, working out new drills and disciplines, retraining the instructors, rewriting the manuals, and a tremendous lot of fuss. Much better to send the officer back to work out a way of winning the battles with the tactics he has already got. All he is trying to do, say the courtiers, is get out of the blame for his defeat by shifting the responsibility onto the system. But after losing a few more battles, they reluctantly admit that hard as it is to change the structure of the army, it is harder still to force the enemy to fight in the way that you have arranged for him to lose.

One of the greatest dangers of listening too hard to the courtier is precisely this, that his advice tends to be influenced, if not dominated, by considerations of internal convenience or the personal prestige of his plan being adopted, not of the success of a whole enterprise. For this reason a king who is happier with his courtiers than with his barons, a chief executive who is happier and more popular with his planning and policy staff than with his next-in-line managers, is always suspect. The circle of courtiers can drift further and further away from reality into the never-never land of Nicholas II; the circle of barons will not—if you have your ear to the ground, you cannot have your head in the clouds. Admittedly you can not see over the next hill, either, so you have to lift your head occasionally, and the value of a good staff to plan and think and look ahead is considerable. But the results of their thoughts and plans must be served up to barons as a tempting refreshment that they can partake of if they choose, not as a medicine that they have to swallow whether they like it or not.

# 19

## THE SUCCESSOR

No one, I suppose, really believes in the hereditary principle any more: It is hard to justify even in theory, and the pages of history are sprinkled with evidence of its failure in practice. What is not quite so clear is whether any other system has produced any better results. It is rather like being able to decide the sex of your children in advance; clearly it ought to be better to have a choice than to be at the mercy of chance, but if you do exercise your choice, there is no certainty that you will be any happier in the long run.

However, the hereditary system, the dynastic system, has disappeared from most states and most corporations, leaving no immediate and obvious solution to the problem of who should take over when the present boss goes. "In elective monarchies," says Gibbon, "the vacancy of the throne is a moment big with danger and mischief." Filling it is probably the most momentous decision that ever has to be taken, or at least the one from which most good and most harm can flow. Sometimes, of course, it is obvious: The future leader has been a marked man for years, standing head and shoulders above his fellows, taking more and more of the responsibility over the past few years, and universally recognized as heir apparent. I would like to believe that such is usually the case, but evidence for this is rather hard to come by. And if there is no obvious successor, what do you do then?

One solution is to leave it to the outgoing leader himself. This will commend itself more if he has been successful than if he has been a failure; but the more successful he has been, the harder it seems to be for him to choose right. I remember Nehru being asked on a British television press conference in the 1950s if he had thought about appointing a successor, and replying that he thought it was not his business: He went on to silence his questioners by adding, "After all, Winston Churchill tried to, and that didn't exactly work out, did it?" It was too early for him to reinforce the point by also citing Macmillan and Douglas-Home, but history has now done so. Perhaps it is not surprising: After all, a good leader has his own vision of where the enterprise should be going and how it should get there, and his idea of a successor is the man most likely to keep going in the same direction. Obviously, this man is probably his closest associate, his number two, the man who has supported him most ably and loyally throughout his career. But the mere fact of having been an able and loyal number two is prima facie disqualification from becoming number one. It suggests someone who is better suited to following than leading, someone whose qualities are complementary to those of the leader instead of identical. A leader will have his own vision, and his own ideas, and they are unlikely to coincide exactly with those of his predecessor; consequently, he may well have antagonized the outgoing leader, or at least questioned his ideas, put up alternatives of his own, and generally created a slight chill in the atmosphere. It therefore takes a very wise man indeed to realize that this thorn in his flesh may make a better successor than the apple of his eye.

Indeed, the more powerful and successful and admired the departing leader, the harder the problem of his successor becomes. To start with, nobody wants a change.

Everything has been going so splendidly that all they want is to keep it running just as it was. And, of course, you can do it for a time. Just as it takes time after a leader's arrival for his influence to become felt, so it takes time after his departure before the effect of his absence is visible; and the bigger the organization, the longer it takes at both ends, because of the greater administrative inertia. Change the only teacher at the village school, and the result may be apparent in a few weeks; change the head of a great university, and it will take years—it will be chiefly noticeable in the kind of men he appoints, and it may take him ten years to appoint enough. But equally, the effect of them will last for years after his retirement. So the impact of a great leader on a big corporation can go on for years after he has gone, and encourage the idea that change is not necessary. Also, if he ruled for long enough, a myth starts to grow around him, so that people begin to act emotionally and illogically from a mistaken belief that they are behaving in a way he would have been proud of. Just as Frederick the Great lost the battle of Jena, so Nelson lost the battle of Coronel in 1914. When Admiral Cradock went to engage Von Spee's crack squadron off the Chilean coast with slower, shorter-range ships carrying less firepower and manned by undertrained men in adverse conditions of light and weather, he was driven on by the spirit of Nelson; but Nelson would never have sought an engagement in those circumstances in a million years. In the same way, the "old man's" fabled risk on what proved to be a highly successful product can pass into the mythology of a firm, so that when a later and far more doubtful product comes up for decision, someone tips the scale by saying, "Old J.B. would have risked it," when old J.B. would not in fact have touched it with a barge pole. And, of course, it is eminently possible for one leader to achieve results that no successor can match; and if he is a dominating, autocratic leader, it makes it even less likely that he will leave the firm with anyone capable of taking over where he left off. Certainly there have been exceptions; the most spectacular was the Roman Emperor Hadrian, who nominated Antoninus Pius to succeed him, on condition that he in turn should immediately adopt Marcus Aurelius as his own successor. "Their united reigns," says Gibbon, "are possibly the only period of history in which the happiness of a great people was the sole object of government."[1] But Hadrian's achievement is almost equally spectacular for its rarity: The list of world-famous figures who left no adequate successor is a formidable one—it includes Cromwell, Bismarck, Napoleon, Genghis Khan, Charlemagne, Attila, and Alexander the Great.

Even if it happens that a good leader is there in the organization, there is no certainty that anyone will think of him. After all, if he has been the critic and the opponent of the revered departed leader, he is not likely to commend himself to his successors. But in such a case there is some compensation, in that he may still be around when trouble comes. If the "old man" was such an autocrat that such critics and opponents were silenced or dismissed, then of course he will have gone. But if he is still there, there is hope. Sweet are the uses of adversity; as long as the afterglow of the old man's reign continues to light up the present, his successors will perhaps seek only ease and comfort, living so to speak off the capital of his achievements. But circumstances change; markets, technology, competition all develop in new ways. The old man might have known how to meet them, but his afterglow is not bright enough to illuminate the path for those who have followed him. As the barometer falls and everyone can see the storm approaching, they stop thinking of comfort and look only for survival. That may mean a different leader: someone who seemed thoroughly unsuitable as a captain for keeping the crew happy and the ship tidily adminis- tered when the weather was sunny and calm, but who, now that shipwreck stares everyone in the face, is admitted to be the only man who can handle the ship in a storm. So at last a good leader may be forced on the firm again in a sort of cycle of triumph and disaster. Walter Bagehot,[2] talking of the government of England, says:

> The great qualities, the imperious will, the rapid en- ergy, the eager nature fit for a great crisis are not required—are impediments—in common times. A Lord Liverpool is better in everyday politics than a Chatham—a Louis Philippe far better than a Napoleon.

Bagehot could not add that Churchill could be a totally unacceptable leader of Britain in 1935 and yet the best possible choice in 1940. It is a question whether Bagehot is right in saying that there are times when you are better served by a humdrum leader than a brilliant one. It may be true, since industrial enterprises can certainly reach a stage when they appear to need only an efficient caretaker. And yet you can never be sure that in ten or twenty years time you will not look back and wish that you had had a man of vision and drive in command then, and many executives believe, or discover to their cost, that the time to change is when everything seems to be going fine. However, Bage- hot's main point is that a system of government needs to be so constituted that the people can quickly change lead- ers if events make a change necessary, and the constitution to be so arranged that the alternative is there for the choos- ing. A corporation does well to let the critical voices be heard, to let an opposition exist, provided it remains within the framework of the constitution, provided it fights just as hard as if it had voted for the war and not against it.

But suppose there is no leader ready to take over in the crisis? If a large firm manages to reach a situation where there is no one of high enough caliber to take over command, it is an awful admission of failure. "Mr. Morgan buys his partners," said Andrew Carnegie; "I grow my own." Nevertheless failure sometimes has to be admitted, particularly if a dreadful crash follows the departure of a repressive, autocratic boss, and bringing in a new boss can appear less of an evil than choosing one of the yes-men who are left.

A new man who is brought in straight after the departure of the autocrat has one great advantage—he inherits a system built to be run by one man. No nonsense about persuasion and diplomacy and delegated authority; it is a one-man show. Perhaps, if he is just as much of an autocrat, he can take up the reins instantly and demonstrate that any stirrings of opposition and independence will get no further than they used to. One of the first actions of Alexander the Great when he succeeded his father, Philip of Macedon, was to crush a revolt in Thebes with extreme brutality, razing the city to the ground, slaughtering six thousand people, and enslaving many more. From then on, the rest of Greece understood that the posture of subjection they had learned under Philip would continue to be appropriate under Alexander. A less brutal but similarly decisive act by an imported boss could have the same effect in teaching his executives that they would do well to keep their kneeling muscles as supple as before.

But the new man may not be a despot, and there are disadvantages to counterbalance the habit of subservience. The resistance to a boss who is brought in from outside can be considerable. He is bound to be considered a poor leader by contrast with the departed paragon, and every change he makes will be considered a change for the worse, since it requires a considerable imagination to conceive that the hallowed practices of ten or twenty years standing may be unnecessary or out of date or wrong. All those who hoped and expected to step into his predecessor's shoes will be violently antagonistic to the man who has robbed them of their rightful inheritance, and the whole firm will feel slighted by the implication that no one within it is good enough to run it. Such resistance may not deter a young Napoleon, but not all leaders are Napoleons, and if he is unwise enough to come alone (see Chapter 23), it could well prove decisive. One man invited in to lead an organization in which most of the senior executives want him to fail is embarking on as demanding a task as you can find.

There is, however, a much more auspicious time to take over. Not while the memory of the former leader is still green and his achievements still bright, but later. Let them appoint a weak leader from within the organization, let him fail, let factions and baronial warfare develop, let morale drop and depression and disgust creep in, and the welcome will change marvelously. The best start that a leader can have is a widespread sense of the need for strong leadership. When the executives start muttering, "If only we had any damn policy at all we'd be fine," "If those idiots upstairs could make up their minds about anything we'd be able to get down to work," "How the hell can I give a production forecast if no one knows what we're supposed to be making?" and finally, "What we need is someone to come in and bang all their heads together"—that is the time for the outsider to step in. It was the aimlessness and corruption of the French Directory that cleared the ground for Napoleon, the division and conflict of the triumvirate that conditioned the Roman Republicans to the dictatorship of Augustus, the exhaustion after interminable baronial wars that made the English willing to accept the stern measures of Henry II (after Stephen), Edward I (after Coeur de Lion and John and Henry III), and Henry VII (after the Wars of the Roses). In that sort of situation, not only are people willing, even anxious, to accept the sort of firmness they would have resisted in more confident times; they are waiting with a halo in their hands for any head that looks worthy to receive it. After the terrors of Mary's reign, the English were passionately willing Elizabeth to succeed, and the doctrine of the divine right of monarchs started to grow up around her, constructed by her subjects as a shield against any rival for her crown. The young Victoria had an almost similar flood of goodwill from a nation disgusted by over a century of gross Hanoverian kings. People in a firm that is badly run, and that knows it is badly run, and whose failure is obvious to all, have banked large sums of loyalty and respect and obedience that they have been unable to spend in the past and are now only too anxious to pour out at the feet of someone who looks as if he deserves them and can use them properly. Of course it may be that he is another autocrat and that the whole cycle will start again, but even that is better than continued decline; and, if you are the new leader, the idea of being remembered as the man who took over a chaotic situation, led a renaissance, retired in triumph, but whose successors could not keep it up, is not absolutely intolerable.

# 20

## *THE EMPEROR*

How do you break the chain? How can you graduate from the elementary system in which a strong king controls the kingdom and rules it well, but the moment a weak king supersedes him it Balkanizes, the barons take over, and you revert to disorder and internecine strife? How do you improve on the firm that is good when the boss is good, but whose shares drop millions of dollars if he dies suddenly? The answer is that you need a man who can do more than rule a kingdom: You need a man who can found an empire.

The qualities necessary to create a kingdom, to build a big firm, are rare enough. The king who can weld together a group of dissident baronies into a single fighting unit, who can win victories and impose his law, or the creative leader who can unite a number of small firms into a disciplined and profitable enterprise, these are exceptional men. And yet they can do all this and it may still fall to pieces again when they depart. What is needed is someone who can build a system that will outlast him; a man who can so devise and organize the internal structure of the kingdom or the corporation that it can survive and remain united despite a humdrum successor. And having created the organization, he needs time; a long enough period of firm government for the new plants to take root and grow strong. It is not as dramatic a role as winning sweeping victories and riding in triumph through Persepolis, but it demands all the creative leader's qualities and in addition a depth of wisdom and understanding that the creative leader can manage without. It is the reason why one Augustus is worth fifty Napoleons.

Two of the classic instances of converting a handful of divisive baronies into an integrated corporate state are Tudor England and General Motors: Both faced the same problem, and both found the same sort of solution. To take Tudor England first; the situation they started from was a nation split by the Wars of the Roses and a long tradition of weak or irresponsible government. Fortunately, there was also sufficient exhaustion and desire for firmness to give Henry VII the chance he needed. He took the first traditional steps of strong kings who succeed weak ones by imposing his authority, removing private armies from the barons, collecting his revenues and filling his treasury, but that alone would not have safeguarded the state. The real work was spread over a longer period, chiefly during the reign of Henry VIII, when the institutions of a modern corporate state were formed to underpin the personal authority of the sovereign. The Court of the Star Chamber is a typical example—an institution that provided for a body of the most powerful men in the kingdom to sit in judgment on any noble, however mighty, who tried to defy the king's authority. Then even if the king was weak, the court was there to impose authority in his name and was composed of men with the power and will to carry it out for him. But there were many other courts and councils and statutes of only slightly less importance, concerned with securing the king's revenue, limiting the jurisdiction of the clergy, improving the administration of justice, and setting the running of the kingdom on a broader base. One of the most important principles was the bringing of top court officials and men of power together in courts and councils to act for the king. His overriding authority was not diminished, but it was reinforced by a group of strong men with an interest in the preservation of law and order and a strong central government. The principle of the distribution of the king's powers, by delegation and not usurpation, over a broader base, of creating institutions whereby the strong men of the land were encouraged to make decisions jointly in the general interest rather than singly in their private interest, was one of the great contributions of the Tudors to the modern state.

The two great councilors of the early Tudor period were Wolsey and Thomas Cromwell. They provide an instructive contrast. Wolsey constantly sought more and more personal power to carry out the king's wishes. Even so, it never seemed quite enough, and when he fell there was not a great deal of his work left behind. Cromwell, on the other hand, was the real architect of the Tudor management revolution.[1] He did not seek personal powers, his aim was constantly to set up new institutions that could then be left to run themselves while he moved on to the next; he instituted courts and councils, giving them authority by legislation and power by their composition, which not only survived his fall but continued, in some instances, right into the nineteenth century, despite a changing society, a developing economy, and a wide variety of subsequent sovereigns. Indeed, perhaps the greatest tribute to the administrative system set up by the Tudors is that it survived the Stuarts.

The Thomas Cromwell of General Motors was Alfred Sloan. Durant, the founder of General Motors, was a medieval king. He gathered together a number of independent baronies—automobile companies, electrical companies, accessory companies—imposed his personal authority on them, but did not weld them into a single state.

It would have been extremely easy to dissolve the cord that bound them and to let them revert to independent companies again. Consequently, when Sloan took over, he found that General Motors was not, in his sense, a company at all. Each operating division—Olds, Cadillac, Chevrolet, Buick, etc.—had its separate bank account into which it paid its earnings and from which it paid its bills: The central administration had just the same difficulty in getting appropriations as medieval kings had in collecting taxes. Each company made the cars it wanted to in the way it wanted to, without confining itself to any planned and concerted range.

Obviously, Sloan could have acted just as a strong medieval king and imposed his will by force. Instead, he built institutions, and set about it in a way astonishingly similar to Cromwell's. Cromwell made the first survey of church property, the *Valor Ecclesiasticus;* Sloan took the first inventory of all General Motors stock in trade. Cromwell had set up and strengthened the Star Chamber to deal with rebellious nobles; Sloan brought the divisional general managers onto the operations committee, to use the combined authority of the barons in upholding a unified policy against any individual who might want to go off on his own. Where Cromwell used the Privy Council, Sloan used the executive committee. Where Cromwell dissolved the monasteries and broke the power of the church, Sloan dissolved the private bank accounts and broke the power of the divisions. Where Cromwell founded the Court of Augmentations for applying church revenues, Sloan formed the finance committee for channeling of capital appropriations. Where Cromwell retained overriding authority for the king, Sloan retained it for the chief executive.

Sloan was an emperor, since he was chief executive himself—both Cromwell and Henry VIII at the same time. He built a system that, like Cromwell's, placed the chief executive's authority on a broader base by bringing in the powerful men of the realm. And his institutions served another purpose: By bringing together all the heads of divisions into central committees, he started "good centralization," a continuous process of education in the central General Motors policy. As the central executives (the court) and the divisional managers (the barons), met week after week on technical committees, finance committees, product planning committees, operations committees, so they tuned in to the central transmitter, and began to share Sloan's vision of what General Motors was, as opposed t ) what Cadillac or Chevrolet was. They were not told what car to produce, what styling to adopt, what engine to include. But when they went back from the emperor's court into their own kingdoms, they had all the parameters within which they could start thinking. They did not try to design a car above a certain price, because they knew another division was doing that. They did not aim at the cheapest possible car in their range, because General Motors aimed at the higher quality in each bracket, even at the expense of a higher price. In St. Augustine's phrase, they were learning to love God, and then doing what they liked.

The emperor is the stage beyond the creative leader, the position that a few creative leaders graduate to, and this ability to found institutions, to create procedures, committees, organizations, and policies that harness the most powerful and influential people to the common cause is the distinguishing feature. But he has another important task; he picks the men. Marcus Wallenberg, the Swedish industrial emperor, said that his greatest value to his kingdoms was in choosing people, in providing them with new kings or potential kings. Someone, after all, has to appoint a chief executive, and the best qualifications for appointing anyone to any job is to have done it successfully yourself. You can only really grade people if you are better than all of them: Only the best physicist in the country can place the top ten in order of merit—number five will be right about the ones below himself, but not necessarily about the ones above himself. And so the emperor is most likely to choose good kings—and not only choose them, but support them and defend them in their early years. It was most important for a king like Horatio Nelson to have an emperor like First Lord of the Admiralty St. Vincent behind him, to choose him in the first place, then to trust him, stick up for him, and defend him against his opponents and detractors. It was invaluable for a king like Drake to have an empress like Elizabeth, who under pressure of international politics could occasionally appear to deplore and disown him while surreptitiously supporting him. The queen herself could not have carried out piratical raids on Spanish ships without grave political implications. But when the Spaniards complained about Drake she could say how shocking it was if true, while taking her share of the prize money on the side. It is also the emperor who can best start colonies, and send men off to found new kingdoms. He can see the market opportunity, choose the man to seize it, and channel the necessary capital toward him. He has graduated from being an entrepreneur to creating an environment in which many entrepreneurs can flourish.

There is a famous circus act in which a juggler starts a plate spinning on a stick, then puts the stick in a slot on a table and starts another plate spinning on another stick, and then a third. By then the first is slowing down, so he rushes and starts it going fast again, and then gets a fourth spinning. Then the second and third need attention, then the first again, then he starts a fifth, and so on until eight plates are spinning and he is moving around keeping them all going. That is one way of looking at the emperor's job: The plates are firms, and the sticks are his chief executives, his kings. He starts up as many enterprises as he can while also giving attention to keeping the existing ones going. If one demands too much of his time, because the stick is too rigid or too flexible, he throws it away and gets another.

The other vital function of the emperor is foreign policy. The industrial emperor is not concerned with driving factories to meet an unexpected sales boom, or urging the salesmen on to get rid of stocks of a product before a rival's improved version reaches the market, or taking over a valuable but shaky supplier. He is looking to the future, to the changing economic and social climate, foreseeing the decline in demand for some products, the rise of others, and opportunities for new ones. He is negotiating with the government, perhaps sitting on government committees, getting wind of proposed legislation, and trying to get additions or modifications considered at the early stages, when it is easier. He is talking to major shareholders, cabinet members, bankers and other industrial emperors, picking up scraps of information that may be invaluable to his kings. He is creating a context and a climate in which they can best govern their kingdoms now and in the years ahead. When the empire is a great industrial empire, turning over billions of dollars, employing hundreds of thousands of people, and creating a significant proportion of the wealth of the Western world, it is a level of responsibility and influence that has few parallels in politics. Thus, students of the twentieth century will find the history of a firm like General Motors a great deal more important than the history of a nation like Switzerland.

# 21

## SPOT THE WINNER

The cream always rises to the top. This happy domestic metaphor can be a great comfort to good corporation men, and the nearer they are to the top, the more comforting they will find it. But not all corporations are milk bottles: Some (if we are to stay in the larder) can be jugs of salad dressing, in which the oil rises to the top and the vinegar stays at the bottom—even if the corporation would be better run by the vinegary executives than by the oily ones. It is, in fact, by no means inevitable that the best men will go to the top of the firm. And even if you pursue the milk metaphor, you will find that cream has another property as well as rising to the top: It also goes sour quickest.

Look inside a great corporation: There are hundreds, maybe thousands, of young or youngish men, who are managers or future managers. Most of them, no doubt, will be reasonably successful, but probably only a handful have it in them to be creative leaders; and yet they are the ones on whom the future growth or decay of the corporation will one day depend. It is therefore of the utmost importance to be able to sort out the few potential winners from the greater mass of intelligent, able, and efficient young men. It is also a great deal harder than it sounds.

The trouble, of course, lies in the numbers. There are so many that the chief executive or members of the board cannot possibly work with them all or get to know them all during their early years, and consequently they depend on the reports they get from the managers they work under. And regrettable as it may seem, the potential leader is often an uncomfortable, and sometimes a disagreeable, subordinate. It is possible that he is of higher caliber than the men he works under, which in itself is hard enough to bear; but he is also unlikely to conceal his perception of this truth, which they find almost unforgivable. When they describe him in formal reports or informal conversations as insolent, egocentric, and argumentative, they are likely to be speaking no less than the truth. They will probably add that he is conceited or arrogant (the difference apparently being that if he thinks he is cleverer than you are, he is conceited, and if he knows he is, he is arrogant). Moreover, if he is already starting to see the corporation as a whole, he is likely to question and criticize policies and decisions that have nothing to do with him or indeed with his immediate superiors, and this can be even more irritating, since they find it harder to argue on unfamiliar territory. He is also likely to have extreme confidence in his own judgment, and this, while invaluable in a creative leader who needs to stimulate morale and enthusiasm among his team, is not a quality that superiors find endearing.

He is not even likely to be obedient—at least not all the time. He will take his own view about the instructions he receives, and will carry them out if he thinks they are reasonable; but if he thinks they are wrong, it will be very difficult to make him comply and go back and tell his own subordinates to do something that he does not believe in. Of course, this is always a problem for intermediate managers: You try to get a bad decision altered, fail, and then have to pass it on to your subordinates. Do you, out of loyalty to the organization, support the decision and let them think you are as stupid as all the rest of them? Or do you sell your superiors down the river, say they are a bunch of buffoons who won't be convinced of their error, and retain the respect of those you have to lead? In the services it is somehow easier: You call them into your office, bark out "C.O.'s instructions: All latrine doors to be painted in diagonal stripes of lilac and vermilion," and they salute and march off to the paint stores. Nobody says anything, but everybody understands. Perhaps you can get away with it in a totally repressive, autocratically run firm, but most firms allow a certain freedom of speech. What does the manager do then? His superiors are in no doubt: Having made his representations to them, he then accepts their decision and passes it on with all his personal authority behind it; when the outburst comes, he simply says "I'm sorry, but there are a great many other factors that you don't know about; I know it seems wrong, but you must take my word that it is the best decision in view of all the other considerations," or words to that effect. Alas, the embryo creative leader cannot be trusted to do the honorable thing. He is quite likely to tell his subordinates exactly what he thinks. Indeed, he has probably already expressed his general opinions about what ought to be done so decisively that, even if he said nothing, they would know exactly what he thought.

The central dilemma is that in a junior management position there is only a certain amount of credit and good will that a person can get, and the more he gets from below the less he gets from above. If he does everything his superiors ask, and accepts all their rulings without demur, those superiors are likely to think him a first-class manager; but his subordinates, who find all their requests refused, their ideas rejected without discussion, rival departments growing at their expense, other people getting better facilities and more pay for less responsibility, will think him a feeble, time-serving *apparatchik*. Conversely, if he quarrels

with every unwelcome ruling, presses vigorously and re-
peatedly for extra scope and pay for his subordinates, and
never takes no for an answer, then while his subordinates
will think him splendid, his superiors will find him a thorn
in their flesh. And it seems to be characteristic of the
creative leader that his personal loyalties are downward
and not upward. His first loyalty is to his own ideas, his
second to the people who he believes will help him realize
them. Both these take a far higher priority than his superiors. Nor is he particularly loyal to the corporation as such;
in so far as it enables him to achieve his objectives, he
accepts and approves of it, but if it requires him to set aside
his objectives, to work as one member of a big team that is
working toward someone else's objective, then he is likely
to lose interest and patience. The Prussian civil service lost
a potentially excellent recruit for this reason: Bismarck
explained the reason for his resignation (in his early twenties) in a letter to a cousin:

> Affairs and official service are utterly uncongenial to
> me; I should not think myself fortunate to become an
> official or even a minister of State; I deem it quite as
> respectable to grow corn as to write despatches, and
> in certain circumstances as more useful; I have more
> inclination to command than to obey. These are facts
> for which I can give no reason beyond my own tastes...
> A Prussian official is like a player in an orchestra. No
> matter whether he be the first violin or the triangle,...
> he has to play his instrument as the needs of the
> concerted piece dictate....But for my part, I want to
> play music such as I regard as good—or else not play
> at all.

Clearly a young graduate recruit to the corporation who
makes it clear that he intends to play such music as he
regards as good, or else not play at all, is not likely to get
the best personal report of his group. Equally clearly, not

many of his temperament would have turned out to be Bismarcks; but if none of them get through, then the possibility of finding any potential Bismarcks is excluded.

Another reason why the potential creative leader is likely to antagonize his superiors is that he is, almost by definition, a bad courtier. One of the constant preoccupations of courtiers is to try to be identified with all successful projects and no unsuccessful ones. Much of their time and ingenuity is spent hedging bets, devising forms of words that will cover them against all eventualities ("Other things being equal, this should work out well—so long as we can be sure that other things will stay equal.") If the enterprise fails, you will find they all advised against it, tried to stop it, warned that this would happen; if it succeeds, you will equally find that each one of them was the one behind it from the start, the one who tilted the balance in its favor, the one who stuck by it when others were weakening. The creative leader is not good at this game: He will have expressed himself far too forcibly on one side or the other from the start, and while if it succeeds he will be one of the many to share the credit, if it fails he will be the only one left with the blame.

Another not very appealing characteristic of the creative leader is that he does not assume that his superiors will make the right decision on questions he refers to them. From time to time, therefore, he will make decisions on his own initiative because he suspects that if he refers them to his superiors, they will decide wrongly. Alternatively he will somehow manage not to see a memo giving him instructions he does not want to follow. "Turning a blind eye" has come to mean deliberately not noticing the misdemeanors of subordinates, but at the Battle of Copenhagen, where the phrase originated, Nelson was the subordinate going out on a limb, ignoring the instruction to break off the engagement issued by Sir Hyde Parker, his superior officer, and risking the most almighty row if he had failed. There is no defense in the event of failure in such a situation, and only grudging forgiveness for success, so it takes considerable self-confidence or a very steady nerve. Even if he turns out to have saved his superiors from disaster, they will not think it was the most lovable way to do it.

For all these reasons, there is a danger that the few potential creative leaders may not rise like cream but be kept down like vinegar—which indeed they resemble more closely. It is only too possible that their immediate superiors will dislike and resent them, report adversely on them, and promote the docile, obedient, easy young executives instead. And, of course, arrogant, egocentric, argumentative behavior is not in itself a guarantee of high potential—the exceptional ability has to be there as well. Rough diamonds can turn out to be rough paste. But it does take considerable wisdom on the part of the senior executive to realize that because this manager is difficult to work over, he is not necessarily difficult to work under and that the unlovable qualities may yet be of greater value to the corporation than the smooth charm of his complaisant contemporaries; and that arrogance, stubbornness, and insubordination are only self-confidence, determination, and initiative with a coating of disapproval. And yet often it is only through his immediate superiors that the top management of the firm receive their reports. It is rather like nurses in a hospital, who are reported on by the nursing supervisor; certainly her report is essential, but there is another additional standard of judgment, namely, the patient's. It is by no means impossible for the best nurse, from the patient's point of view, to be the worst from the supervisor's point of view, and vice versa. The supervisor's ideal may keep everything tidy and sterile, always be swift, efficient, and punctual, and leave the patients frightened, depressed, and unhappy; the other may keep the whole ward cheerful and contented, but give them the wrong drugs from time to time. The point is that both these judgments are relevant, while the former is the only one that will be passed on. In the same way there is often another view of the young creative leader, which may never be made known.

The solution adopted by some military commanders—certainly General Horrocks[1]—is to establish the practice whereby the man directly responsible for the job reports to the commander, the chief executive; not on routine matters, but when there is an emergency, when the pressure is on, or when important plans are being formulated or results analyzed. It may mean only two conversations a week, of fifteen minutes each, with junior officers or managers, but that is still meeting a hundred a year; and not socially, on good behavior, but operationally, under testing conditions in which lucidity, intelligence, knowledge, judgment, and independence are all called on. Horrocks always invited the man's superior officer to be present if he wished, to show that it was not a going-behind-the-back operation. The advantage is not just a chance for the chief executive to make up his own mind about the quality of the younger managers, but also to get authentic information and appraisals and proposals directly from the man who generated them and not filtered through a number of barons and courtiers.

It is harder to know just how the young potential leader himself should behave toward a superior who is likely to block his proposals, reject his ideas, and frustrate his plans. The only practical advice I know of was intended for a rather different situation, namely, what you should do if you are walking in the jungle and you meet a lion. If you turn and run, it will chase you by instinct; if you move toward it and corner it, it will leap at your throat out of fear. What you must do is advance on it steadily and confidently, but make sure to leave it a way out, a line of retreat. Then, as you get too near for comfort, it will turn around and slink away. In other words, however bitter his row with his superior, he must always leave him a way open to consent without climbing down: he must keep back a significant fact or an alternative proposal or a reasonable modification until his superior realizes the strength of determinations he is up against, just as Kennedy did in the Cuban missile crisis. Then, when the lion starts to look around for a track through the jungle, the escape route is ready for him to slink down.

# 22

## GRESHAM'S LAW OF MANAGEMENT

It is a perennial lament of the industrial corporations that not enough graduates apply to join them, and that those who do apply are not the best. Various reasons are advanced, usually implicitly blaming the universities for instilling the wrong standards, or the graduates for having no ambition; sometimes the corporations look inward at themselves, wondering in a puzzled way whether they have the wrong image, a sort of B.O. of the reputation, and mount an expensive public relations campaign to treat this ailment (ads in the college magazines, glossy brochures, film shows on the campus, conducted tours) to try to win graduates and influence Ph.D's. But all too often they find, like those who fall for the deodorant advertisements, that it was not B.O. at all. They were simply unattractive, and they still are.

Not that industry is intrinsically unattractive to graduates: The trouble lies in the difference between what they want and what the corporations are actually offering them. The corporation says in effect, "Come and join us. We have any number of interesting posts for young people like you. Our research activities range from metallurgy through molecular biology to astrophysics; we have vacancies in sales, advertising, data processing, personnel; we have plants and offices all over the country and in forty other countries around the world; there is bound to be a niche for you somewhere. We offer you a well-paid, secure career with medical benefits, travel concessions, and a pension scheme. Our shares are riding high, our growth record is impressive, our name is a byword for quality all around the world. What more can you want?" But it is not a question of wanting more—if anything, they want less. They are not, many of them, interested in security, pensions, and range of possibilities; they are interested in the one specific job that they themselves will be doing when they start. And that is the one thing they are hardly ever told. They are being asked to commit themselves to an institution for life without knowing whom they will work with or what they will do, and they are far too bright to be taken in by the admen's adjectives like "exciting," "challenging," "expanding," which are sprinkled over the brochures. I know an extremely intelligent, lively, enterprising graduate who passed up all the corporations to join a shaky outfit with a staff of four, which offered him no pension, no health scheme, and a real possibility that the firm might fold up in six months. But they told him exactly what he would have to do—namely, start up and run the whole sales operation—and he could see how he might make it work. It may be presumptuous of a young graduate to want to run something on his own, but some of the best of them do and not in the fullness of time, after progressing through a probationary period, but starting on Monday morning. Bismarck, in the letter quoted in Chapter 21, went on to say:

> For a few renowned statesmen, especially in countries with an absolute constitution, patriotism has been the motive driving them into the public service; much more often, the mainspring has been ambition, the wish to command, to be admired, to be famous. I must admit that I myself am not free from this passion. Many distinctions, such as those which accrue to a soldier in wartime, or to a statesman under a free

constitution, to such men as Peel, O'Connell, Mirabeau, etc.—men who had their part to play in energetic political movements—would exert on me an attractive force which would override every consideration, would lure me as a flame allures a moth. I am less attracted by successes which I might secure along trodden roads, by examinations, influence, the study of documents, seniority, the favor of my superiors.

The Bismarck instinct may be all wrong for the organization man, but it is right for the leader. The only real training for leadership is leadership: You do not learn it by being an assistant or a deputy, only by being a boss.

The advice Peter O'Toole gave to Michael Caine was that if he wanted to be a leading actor he must only play leading parts: much better to play Hamlet in Denver than Laertes on Broadway. In the same way, the best way to learn how to lead a big organization is by leading smaller ones, and this is the one thing the great corporation does not offer.

I do not believe this has to be so. I believe that in addition to all the nice comfortable posts that the corporation offers to the graduates in search of a secure career for life at twenty-one, it could devise jobs for the others as well. It could say, "We are installing new machine tools in four of our factories; we have a bulk trade-in offer for the old ones of 20 percent of the price we paid four years ago. We think we could get more—say thirty-three or forty—if we went out and sold them directly to users. That's your job. Set it up as you like, and keep X percent on all sales in your department. When you can afford it, recruit some more of your friends. If you're not getting anywhere in six months, that's it. There's no security, no pension, no fixed salary; no boss either, only an auditor. If you really get it running, you could be earning $50,000 a year, in a couple of years, and there's all our old trucks and vans to think about as well. If you don't, well, you're only twenty-one, you'll find another job easily enough. Off you go." I suspect that there are a number of small ways of earning money that it is not economic for a corporation to bother about, but that a bright young man with an eye for the main chance could turn to his profit and theirs.

Otherwise, if the corporation is only offering a secure future disguised as an exciting challenge, it is in danger of being overweighted with recruits whose primary concern is the pension plan, and then Gresham's law will start to operate. The bad drives out the good in management as well as in currency: If a man looks around him and sees people whom he recognizes as less able than himself all doing more or less the same work for more or less the same salary, he will start to think he is in the wrong place. As soon as he sees one or two of them promoted above him, he will know it. I sometimes suspect that the tremendous significance of promotions and appointments is not fully realized in the corporations. You can issue directives and policy statements and messages to staff until the wastepaper baskets burst, but they are nothing compared with promotions. Promotions are the one visible, unmistakable sign of the corporation's standard of values, an irrevocable declaration of the qualities it prizes in its staff, a simultaneous warning and example to everyone who knows the nature of the job and the qualities of its new incumbent. Men who have worked diligently and successfully and then see those who have worked less diligently and less successfully promoted above them start to read the management want ads in the paper the following morning. Gresham's law operates more swiftly and inexorably through bad promotions than by any other agency. And, of course, it can multiply fast: Inadequate men perpetuate their own inadequacy by the appointments and promotions they make in their turn. Men tend to value most highly the qualities they believe themselves to possess, as Bertrand Russell points out when accounting for the disastrous appointments made by President Jackson:

> After all, he had been a successful judge without knowing the law, and a successful General without studying strategy or tactics; it was therefore only natural that he should regard a good heart rather than a good head as affording the right qualification for public position.[1]

Another powerful deterrent to the potential leaders who do join is often constructed by the corporations themselves. It is called the grading system, and is another instrument of Gresham's law. It is not particularly damaging, so long as it is flexible, for clerical and secretarial posts, but the higher the post the more questionable the whole system becomes. The principle is that you grade all the jobs in the corporation, state what the duties and responsibilities are, attach a salary scale to each grade with a little leeway for the exceptional people, and all your personnel worries are over. Perhaps it would work in a completely static organization; the fallacy lies in the assumption that jobs are not changed in status importance and value by the people who are doing them, whereas in fact a post that is fairly insignificant when filled by A can be so expanded in importance by B that the grading becomes ridiculous. However, B is shackled to a salary scale by the grade, and it takes a major operation to increase it, by which time B may well have left. The implied assumption that all people of about the same seniority are worth about the same has a Gresham effect because the best believe they are worth a great deal more than the average, whereas the average and subaverage are perfectly happy and are often paid above their value because of the violent agitation of the best people. But the fact of having to drag the whole of their grade with them in a pay raise makes any significant increase out of the question; and a large increase would put them into a higher grade and cause a riot among men of greater seniority. There is no absolute reason why salary should be shackled to status, but under the grading system it is more or less inevitable. It makes it almost impossible to give adequate payment to a successful creative leader who starts to build an ordinary sort of job into something really impressive and valuable.

The process can also fail the other way. If you insist on paying the post and not the man, you have to keep upgrading the post when a first-class man fills it. But his successor may be much less able, and cannot possibly keep up to the standards of his predecessor—the mantle of Elijah falls upon Elisha and damned near suffocates him. Obviously, the mantle ought to be cut down to size immediately, but once a post has been upgraded with all the consequent trouble, no one is ever particularly anxious to downgrade it again.

The alternative is to pay people according to your judgment of their quality, and their price, like a share price, will take account of their growth potential and their likely future yield, as well as their book value. After all, the work of the corporation is in practice man-oriented and not post-oriented: Research projects are not decided according to the grades of the posts in the research department, but according to the actual abilities and knowledge and interests of the actual people in the department. Joe Hyman of Viyella International had, in principle, no posts in his organization. Mr. Jones was called Mr. Jones, and Mr. Smith was called Mr. Smith. If Mr. Smith happens to be handling press matters he can call himself press officer if he wants to, but only for his dealings outside the firm; the title is like a company umbrella that he picks out of the rack on his way out of the building if it's raining. He remains plain Mr. Smith when he is inside. His salary is not the press officer's salary, it is Mr. Smith's salary, and his duties are Mr. Smith's. If he happens to be marvelous at taking the minutes of the board, there's no nonsense about the press officer doing the company secretary's job. He's just Mr. Smith, and that's what Mr. Smith is going to do today.

The real attraction of the grading system, I suspect, has nothing to do with the efficiency of the corporation. There is no difficulty about treating each manager's salary separately according to his value as an employee rather than according to some arbitrary and out-of-date decision on the grade of his post; a small firm can do it easily, and nearly all of them do. No, the beauty of the grading system is that the administrators can hide behind it during those awkward interviews when staff want to know why they are not being paid more, and in particular why they are not being paid as much as someone else. As long as you have a grading system, you can talk about special demands of the post and keep it all polite. Take it away, and you have to come clean and say, "Because, highly as we value you, we value him even more highly." You have to admit the awful reality that some people may be more valuable to the firm than others by virtue of their nature instead of by virtue of the job they happen to be doing. Even, perhaps, that a younger lower-ranking man may be worth more than his senior. And that might mean that some of the less successful staff might leave out of pique. The alternative of letting Gresham's law drive out the most successful through frustration, and prevent other promising recruits from ever joining, seems somehow easier to bear.

# 23

## *THE GENERAL*

"Commerce is like war," says Walter Bagehot.[1] "Its result is patent. Do you make money or do you not make it? There is as little appeal from figures as from battle." It is indeed so like war that every stage of military history has its parallel in industrial and commercial warfare. Of course, you have to make certain transferences: Territory is share of the market, not acreage of land; where soldiers went out to fight with swords or muskets, sales representatives go out with samples and specifications and discounts; victory is not decided by which army is left in possession of the field, but by which firm sells more of its product. Instead of laying down an artillery and aerial barrage just before sending in the infantry, you lay down a press and broadcasting barrage just before sending in the sales representatives. Instead of military spies stealing battle plans, industrial spies steal engineering designs.

The changing tactics and developing technology of war have their parallel in almost every industry: Where Napoleon evolved a military tactic of flexible, skirmishing troops to overthrow the rigid battle lines of the other European armies, so General Motors evolved a graduated range of cars to overthrow the rigid, single-price line of Model T's; where nations have had to graduate from bombers to missiles and antimissile missiles just because the

enemy had them or might have them, so electronic manufacturers have had to graduate from vacuum tubes to
transistors and to microprocessors for the same reason. Just
as armies adapt their weapons and tactics to different
terrains, so firms adapt their product and sales pitch to
different markets.

Moreover, in industry as in war, size and wealth are
not enough in themselves to guarantee victory. Sixteenth-
century Spain was far larger and richer than England, but
the Armada still lost. This is not to say that England could
have conquered Spain—manifestly she could not—only
that she could not be dislodged from her share of the
market. Her product (the British fleet) was absolutely right
for her section of the market (naval warfare and defense
against invasion). Had she tried to employ her vastly inferior army in a full-scale continental war against Spain, she
would have been destroyed in no time.

There is also guerrilla warfare. At a time when an
American data processing firm had no equipment to compete with IBM, it sent a small group of salesmen across the
states simply to sow the seeds of doubt and discontent and
resentment in the minds of existing IBM users. It was
selling nothing, but IBM area managers all over the country
spent weeks after the visit of the guerrillas soothing ruffled
customers, explaining away all the real or fictitious defects
and limitations they were complaining about, and never
having a moment to go out and sell anything to anyone. It
was a classic piece of guerrilla warfare—maximum damage with minimum resources.

But of all the parallels between war and industry, the
most consistently instructive is that between generalship
and leadership. Imagine an industrial general whose force
has been selling, very successfully, against a much larger
and wealthier competitor. Say the product is a fairly expen-

sive sports car. And then the competitor brings out a cheaper competitive model—better performance and more up-to-date—which topples their sales drastically. But just as the salesmen wonder where the next month's bonus is coming from, out comes their own firm's brand-new model aimed at a different, less wealthy market, where it will obviously have a guaranteed sale for years. The salesmen realize that the defeat of the previous model had been foreseen well in advance, and the new one had been prepared long before as a safe line of defense. Clearly such generalship builds confidence and morale that will be invaluable in the future and a willingness on the salesmen's part to do whatever they are told simply because they know they can trust their leader. This was almost exactly what happened at Torres Vedras in 1810: Wellington's army, after considerable success against the French in Portugal, finally had to withdraw from Bussaco. For ten days they marched back toward Lisbon, their morale dropping after their previous successes against Napoleon's "invincible" army, and the French in close pursuit all the time. And then on the tenth day they came to the mountains of Torres Vedras, and could hardly believe their eyes. There, empty and waiting for them, was an impregnable defensive position: trenches, parapets, palisades, forts, redoubts; scores of guns perfectly disposed, covering trees felled and hollows filled in, streams dammed to create marshes to trap attackers; fifty miles of earthworks in depth, which it must have taken a year to design and build. The soldiers realized that the retreat had been foreseen a year ago, that it was all part of the plan. It is not surprising that Wellington's army was a firm that did not have a morale problem.

No doubt few marketing managers or chief executives see themselves as Wellingtons or their rivals as Massenas, and no doubt they are right not to. And yet much of their work demands exactly the qualities that used to be the preserve of generals. It is a common misconception to think that great generalship is all tactics and battleground decisions. The real job of a general, which takes years, is to build an army into a first-rate force. Nelson was certainly a brilliant tactician, but equally certainly he could not have got his results without the disciplinary system instilled into the navy by St. Vincent. Wellington, too, owed a huge debt to the Light Division trained over a long period by Sir John Moore. In the same way, the real test of management is not just a particular decision, vital though it may be, but building a really efficient firm over the years. There can be no swift solution: If an army gets a simple new weapon, the enemy can copy it quickly and cancel it out. If it takes a long time, like inventing and setting up production of the tank, it will last much longer. In just the same way a firm that finds a quick solution will find it quickly copied: It is the slow and painstaking building up of teams of skilled people and a body of scientific and technological experience that is the basis for a lasting success, because no one will be able to copy it for so long that few will even try.

Another characteristic shared by successful generals and successful industrial leaders is the urge to get the initiative. There are times when this is an unattainable luxury, when survival alone is difficult enough, and all leaders need to master the defensive arts. In any conflict—industrial, commercial, political, military—the first necessity is to be able to stave off disaster. The possession of this quality does not guarantee success, but the lack of it guarantees failure. The leader is distinguished from the others in that he is always aiming for the position where he dictates the moves from his own will and in pursuit of his own aims, and not in answer to the moves of others. There have been many generals whose only strategy has been to wait and see what the other general does and then counter it; there have been many firms whose policy has been to see what their rivals do and then copy it. They are governed not by an ultimate objective but by a series of conditioned reflexes.

It is interesting to see the logic of good generalship forcing itself on management. One of the principles of conducting a battle well is that the general should get "the smell of the battlefield"; it is not enough, they say, for him to sit in his command headquarters receiving reports and issuing orders, as if the whole thing was an academic exercise. He must get around, hear the junior commanders' reports on the spot, talk to the men who have been in the front line, catch the tone of their voice and the look in their eyes, learn the rapidity and weight of the enemy bombardment by actually watching the shells burst. Equally when Britain's leading chain store, Marks and Spencer, had their "good housekeeping" administrative revolution in 1956, it was on exactly these lines: Head office staff, it was decided, cannot function by reading returns from the stores, and pouring over graphs and charts and tables of figures, and then making decisions. They must go around and get the smell of the stores, talk to the managers and the clerks on the counter, note where customers are bunched and where they are sparse, overhear their remarks, look at the expressions on their faces, in fact see the battle in progress for themselves.

Perhaps the most striking difference between the industrial and the military general, apart from the kind of battle they fight, is in the size of their armies. The allegiance of the army has often been a decisive factor in the history of states, and the general who could march on the capital with the army behind him was the effective ruler. The army in a big corporation is smaller, but it can be any group under a single man who could cripple the firm by all walking out together. In one case it might be the marketing team; in another, the research group; it is the ones who know they would be snapped up by all the other firms in the business. It is why senior managers thinking of changing firms are so often asked, "Whom can you bring with you?" It is good to recruit a general, but better to recruit an army, and the leader who joins a rival's research department with eight key people can inflict as much damage on the firm he leaves, both by the weakness he creates and the strength he gives to the other side, as any army that goes over to the enemy; as when a key group of computer designers left Sperry Rand and founded the Control Data Corporation. In fact, of course, most industrial armies march on the capital: The corporation general uses the leverage power his army gives him as a sanction in his bargaining with the government, and when he asks for the facilities, money, policies, and, priorities he wants, it is tacitly understood what damage he can inflict if he does not get them. The favorite device of governments, of course, is to remove the general from the army, and bring him into court. If the head of the research and development division is brought onto the board, it can mean more money and status, but still break his power. Gradually, some of his team will disperse to other jobs in the firm, a new head will take over (or one of the team will be promoted) and the danger of a walkout will have gone. Then the arrogant, assertive general can be disciplined and confined. His army may not be quite the force it used to be, but that is a small price to pay for removing such a great danger.

Julius Caesar, of course, had the right answer. He broke all the rules by bringing his army across the Rubicon and into Rome. Consequently, the recalled general became the master of the state. In the same way, an industrial general can take his army with him. Robert McNamara went to Ford in 1946 with a group of ten officers who had worked together on statistical control and organizational problems in the Air Force; they sold themselves as a package, and when he became president that package formed his army, the small but highly respected and trusted group through whom he ruled. Similarly, when he was appointed defense secretary, he went to the Air Force's RAND Corporation for a group of high-powered executives to form his army to fight the Pentagon barons. Alone, he would almost certainly have been run by the admirals and generals and permanent officials. With the RAND group, he could run them. Within a corporation, the general who is moved into court will sometimes bring his army with him—accept the directorship, but retain executive control of his old division at the same time, and perhaps also bring two or three of his old team into head office as assistant directors reporting to him. More often, of course, it happens by consent: The most powerful general in the firm is wanted as managing director anyway, and if he wants to bring a couple of his most trusted subordinates with him, no one minds. Then the research and development division is likely to become the Praetorian Guard. In Rome, they were a military elite in especially close contact with the emperor. A commission in the Praetorian Guard was a step to high place, even though the rank itself might be low compared with senior officers in other legions, and the guard could at times force the choice of a new emperor. Most corporations have a Praetorian Guard—a division or department that, on the face of it, is just one among many, but that in fact is generally known to be in a special relationship with the chief executive and that is considered a proving ground or grooming stable for the top executives of the future. And, like Rome's Praetorian Guard, it is usually admitted, however grudgingly, to be a highly effective and able group. More to the purpose, from the general's point of view, is the fact that they owe their allegiance directly to him, and their presence in the palace with their loyal hearts, strong arms, and sharp swords is a safeguard against the political intriguers in high places who might otherwise be plotting a palace revolution.

# 24

## RISK AND RESTRAINT

If you can make one heap of all your winnings
And risk it on one turn of pitch-and-toss,
And lose, and start again at your beginnings
And never breathe a word about your loss…

—Rudyard Kipling[1]

He either fears his fate too much,
Or his deserts are small,
That puts it not unto the touch,
To win or lose it all.

—Marquis of Montrose[2]

These noble sentiments are probably the best recipe for disaster in running a great enterprise. It is noticeable how the famous and successful commanders have almost always tried to avoid making a heap of all their winnings and risking them on anything. Wellington, Nelson, Marlborough, Montgomery, despite the glamorous, dashing aura that surrounds their names, always tried to make sure that they were not risking more than they could afford to lose, and were prepared to break off whenever a calculated risk appeared to be moving beyond their calculations. It was the reason why Jellicoe at Jutland could not put it to the touch, could not risk the destruction of the British fleet in trying to destroy the German fleet; success would not have imperiled Germany nearly as much as failure would have imperiled Britain. The British fleet was the stronger, the greater enterprise, and in those circumstances you do not stake more than you can afford to lose.

It is a very different matter if you are at the other end of the scale. Then, if there is a great jackpot to be won, it does not signify that the odds may be enormously against you—the dream of it is enough; at least it is enough to keep millions of people buying their lottery tickets week after week for most of their lives. This practice is generally regarded as an amiable weakness, but it may be a much more significant symptom of a weak economy and fear of unemployment, because the jackpot is about the only jackpot left.

A manager friend of mine was recently on a trip to America. When he was in the airport lounge, a stranger rushed up to him. "You're from England?" he said.

"Yes—are you?"

"Used to be. Living over here now. Where do you come from?"

"Cobham."

"Oh God, how marvelous. I used to live on Epsom Downs. Loveliest place in the world."

"But presumably you like it better here?"

"I loathe it here."

"Then your wife likes it better?"

"She hates it."

"Then you're earning a lot more than you were?"

"The hell I am. I'm working harder and earning less."

"Well, why stay here, for God's sake? Why not come back with us?"

"I'll tell you why. Because I've got a feeling here," and he started slapping the back of his head violently, "that tomorrow I'm going to hit the jackpot. I haven't hit it in eleven years, but I still feel I could hit it tomorrow. And it's a feeling you can't get in Britain. That's why I'm not coming back."

No jackpots. No incentive for the man who is prepared to stake his time, his unremitting efforts, and his small savings in the hope of winnings on a grand scale. It can be a terrible cause of national lethargy and complacency. The reason is this: Large states and large corporations have an interest in the status quo. They make accommodations with each other, they have gentlemen's agreements, they settle for a fair return on capital and an easy life. They agree not to poach staff, to pay comparable wages, to charge similar or identical prices, to narrow the areas of damaging competition. The giants of the oil industry aim not at wars of conquest but at a balance of power. The giants of the United States electrical industry in the 1950s even agreed the percentages—GE, 45; Westinghouse, 35; Allis-Chalmers, 10; Federal Pacific, 10. Obviously, this can lead to lethargy and stagnation, to the slow growth of inefficiency. The force that stops this is the small, growing, thrusting firms, each fighting against perhaps only one product or in one area, but each capable of exposing any failure or weakness of an area manager or product manager of the big corporations, and keeping him on the tips of his toes. Rome may not be threatened, but if the centurion on the frontier loses two forts to a tribe of badly armed but fierce and cunning Dacians, then he's probably had it. And it is that, much more than the general's annual inspection and report, that forces him to keep his men fit and alert. And if the whole frontier is ringed with tribes like the Dacians, the Roman army will be a lean and muscular organization. If it is only guarding the seashore against enemies without navies, that is when the rot is likely to set in.

The trouble is that all the advantages are with the big army or the big corporation. The small tribes and firms have to put in three times the effort and ingenuity, and take ten times the risk, for the same share of the market. And this usually comes down to one man, to the tribal leader, the entrepreneur. And why should he? He will have to work all day and most of the night and risk his life's savings; and for what? If there's a jackpot, then OK. But not for a 9 percent return on his capital if he succeeds, and ruin if he fails. Only a big profit, an obscene profit, would make such risks and such work worth undertaking.

Every day in the 1960s, evidence of this lack of jackpots in Britain was literally brought to my doorstep. The three big milk retailers in London had carved the city into zones, in which they did not compete with each other. The choice was simply between the one that had your zone, and the Cooperative Wholesale Society's milk route. Both, in my area, were extremely unpopular—it had been a regular source of neighborhood irritation for years. They came late, they never had cream, but they were always trying to sell you cakes and butter and other things your grocer did better, and they were impervious to complaints. It was an ideal situation for an enterprising operator to start up his own firm—he could capture a third of the market in a month, with everyone's gratitude. But no one did. I do not think this is because Britain is an unenterprising nation; I think it is the structure of taxation, the licenses and formalities, that deter the entrepreneur from bothering. It's simply that there is no jackpot.

You might, I suppose, formulate a rule that the acceptable odds become shorter as the enterprise becomes larger: Where a man on his own can risk everything on a 50-1 against chance, a great corporation needs at least 50-1 on. The weakness in such formulas is that you can never compute the odds, and all too often you do not know how much you are risking when you start. There are even instances where leaders have laid unspecified sums at uncertain odds without knowing the prize money either. Perhaps the only consideration that makes such a risk possible is the insidious one of prestige—the current synonym for glory (or vanity, depending on how you look at it). If the ego of the chief executive is harnessed to a project, the conference table can turn into a gaming table before he realizes it. It was prestige that lured the kaiser into a risk he could not possibly have calculated at the time when he decided to build a battle fleet, and thereby turned Britain irrevocably against Germany. The tactical and strategic advantages were small; it was prestige that drove him on, the feeling that a nation as great as he intended Germany to be "ought" to have a fleet. Britain is great: Britain has a fleet. Germany must be great: Germany must have a fleet. The equation was as simple as that. You might think that a corporation with the logic of the balance sheet and the pressures of shareholders would be free from such *folie de grandeur;* but are they? RCA decided to go in for computers—because they needed to for the future? Or because they were the great electronics firm, so they "ought" to sell great computer systems because IBM did? Whatever the reason, they must have realized that, quite apart from the gamble on what it would cost and if and when it would pay off, they were inviting IBM and other established computer firms to try to stop them, as the kaiser invited the British Empire to come and stop him.

This is not to say that prestige is never worth a risk—the question is, prestige for what? When Bismarck embarked on the war against Austria, it was a prestige operation, but prestige with a purpose: to make the German states unite around Prussia's success. He also demonstrated his awareness of a principle that escapes many modern governments, namely, that a merger of equals does not work: There must always be a dominant partner around whom the others cluster as a promise of success or at least a hope of averting failure, and even though faces may be saved in public, everyone must know privately that there is a single leader. When governments try to "rationalize" an industry in which none of the firms acknowledge a single leader, they are asking for trouble. Talleyrand speculated of Napoleon in 1800:

> Two roads are open to him—the federal system which leaves each ruler, after his defeat, still master in his own territory on conditions favorable to the victor, but on the other hand, does he intend to unite and to incorporate? If so he will enter on a course to which there is no end.

A government can perhaps enforce a federal system on an industry, but that rarely solves anything. To unite and incorporate is another matter, and without a willingness on the part of all to accept the leadership of one, it is likely to be beyond the power of most governments.

All this, of course, is not to say that risks should not be taken; only that the notion of risking everything on one throw is a romantic fallacy. The hallmark of the great generals, the Wellingtons and Marlboroughs and Nelsons, has been their extreme skill in working out the risk. They really seem to have anticipated S.J. Simon's advice to bridge players,[3] namely, to work out before any bid or play the answers to three questions:

> How much can this win?
> How much can it lose?
> What are its chances of success?

And, of course, if you know your job, your men, your opponent, and your terrain better than anyone else, you can calculate the odds with more precision. Many business risks have looked much bigger than they were because the man who took them knew things that were guesswork to others: Chances they thought were even, he knew were 3-1 in his favor. There is one other factor, omitted by Simon, that is true of bridge, industry, and war, and that is the valuable stretching effect of a risk that looks as if it will not quite come off. Many of the most brilliant performances at bridge have been brought out of players who were playing in a contract one trick higher than their hands warranted. The extra effort and concentration demanded of them actually improved them as players. In the same way, suppose an army plans a campaign to knock out a troublesome neighbor. They win the battle but do not destroy his army, and find themselves with an open flank. They take violent and urgent action to secure it, rushing up reinforcements and advancing to a line of distant hills for a defensive position. By superhuman effort prompted by self-preservation, they succeed, holding their front and securing their flank. They then realize that they have done more than knock out a troublesome neighbor—they have actually enlarged their kingdom. Similarly a plastics firm producing raw materials went into a new line, in case their competitors got ahead of them. They then found it was not very profitable, through lack of uses that buyers could find. So they started a factory to make roofing materials and partition walls with it so as to (1) take their surplus and (2) demonstrate its qualities as a salable commodity. This succeeded, and they found themselves in a new business as well as succeeding in the old one. Again it was the partial success of the gamble, threatening consequent dangers, that forced the hard thought and urgent action that is now paying off so handsomely.

And just as there may be advantages in the risks that do not quite come off, so there can be grave danger in the ones that come off completely. The greatest danger lies in the difficulty of stopping. You raise and train a great army, build a munitions industry to supply it, instill the principles of attacking warfare into your generals, and then march against your enemy. You win: What do you do then? You have a victorious army, dreaded commanders, a thriving industry: Do you disband it all? With another country ripe for the conquering? Of course not. So off you go. And if you succeed again, it becomes even harder to stop. Besides, if you are vain and egocentric—and you almost certainly are—you begin to dream extravagant dreams. In the same way, if you raise capital, build and equip factories, train a labor force and a sales force, and then go out and sell with great success, you find the same pressure for further conquest, under the name of growth or expansion, throbbing inside your head. You dream of your firm moving up into the big league, dominating world markets, and of yourself as one of the great international tycoons. And that, in industry and war, is the danger point. Hitler and Napoleon both crossed it spectacularly, each in the end taking on greater military commitments than he could meet. In commercial terms, they ran into a classic cash-flow crisis: They could not support their own expansion. In industry the cases are less famous but more frequent.

It is not only the fact of growing too fast that brings about the downfall of the winner who cannot leave the tables; it is also the wall of enmity and passionate desire for revenge that he creates in his opponents. They are prepared to go to extreme limits, they fight like men locked in personal combat to the death. It is obvious in a Hitler or a Napoleon, less obvious in industry; but a rival firm that takes a great knock, so that shareholders clamor, directors shout and thump the desk, and salesmen's bonuses tumble drastically, is a firm spurred to superhuman efforts, willing to work and sweat like never before, willing to form alliances with all the others—and the bankers as well—to bring down this one great threat to everyone's security.

It is interesting to note how two of the great founders of lasting empires—Augustus and Bismarck—were both acutely aware of this danger. Augustus (after burning his fingers) laid it down as a rule for himself and all his successors that the Roman Empire must stop at the Danube. Cross it, and the risks were not calculable, the drain on the resources of the rest of the empire might be catastrophic. Bismarck also believed in the limited objective; he could easily have conquered the Baltic states, but he refrained. He could have humiliated Austria, but instead he ended a brief war with a generous peace that simply secured his original objective of uniting the German states under Prussia, and keeping Austria reasonably friendly. He was urged to build a battle fleet, but refused. In all his plans he had a limited objective, and he halted when he reached it.

The act of deciding what you do not want, what business you are *not* in, at what point you will stop, is less glamorous than marching on from one opportunistic triumph to the next. Nevertheless, it sorts out the emperors from the kings. Simon Marks, of Marks and Spencer, was constantly under pressure to expand: He was running nearly 240 chain stores with spectacular success—why didn't he double the number? Why didn't he go into Europe? Why didn't he export in bulk to the United States? The answer, quite simply, was that for him all those courses were a form of crossing the Danube. He could see how his 240 stores could continue to be competitive, continue to produce quality goods for the mass market, continue to provide steady growth and a good return on capital employed for many years ahead. Move beyond that, and the risk could not be calculated. Perhaps the greater knowledge and broader vision of a successor could encompass such expansion, but he preferred to stay within his frontiers, letting his existing stores expand their selling area in a satisfactory but moderate way. In a smaller way, Mothercare started up in Britain in the 1960s, selling everything for expectant mothers and for children up to three years old. But they did not really take off until they made the decision to bring down the limit from three years to two years. Again, it was the decision to stay out of a market that was the foundation of success.

The concept of growth as a necessity is at the moment unchallengeable. It is an assumption that lies at the root of so much thinking, so many decisions and plans, that even if you could prove the concept false no one could afford to believe your proof. All the same, we can still analyze it, we can separate the steady increase of the world's wealth from the zero sum, the growth of one firm at the expense of another with no overall increase in wealth to match. Self-restraint, said Bismarck, is the mark of the statesman. Already, in great industries like oil, invisible lines are being drawn on nonexistent maps, existing shares of the market are tacitly accepted; if oil is the Europe of modern industry, then the frontiers are becoming more or less accepted—barring the odd skirmish—and most of the shooting warfare is confined to the Balkans of the very small companies. Growth will go on, but maybe self-restraint is starting to creep in as well.

# 25

## RELIGION AND THE CORPORATION

A corporation, like a state, needs a faith. Most people gain comfort from the feeling that they are in some way doing good, helping mankind, leaving the world a better place, serving a noble ideal; and a corporation that enables its employees to feel that they are doing all those things by virtue of their job is clearly onto a good thing. Just as soldiers fight much better for a great cause like Christianity or Liberty or Democracy than for the protection of trading interests, so insurance firms can put more pressure on sales representatives who feel they are spreading protection and security and peace of mind among their fellow citizens than ones who simply believe they are being paid to increase the company's return on employed capital and the annual dividends of the shareholders. As Walter Bagehot says:[1]

> No orator ever made an impression by appealing to men as to their plainest physical wants, except when he could allege that those wants were caused by someone's tyranny. But thousands have made the greatest impression by appealing to some vague dream of glory, or empire, or nationality. The ruder sort of men—that is, men at one stage of rudeness—will sacrifice all they hope for, all they have, *themselves*, for what is called an idea—for some attraction which seems to transcend reality, which aspires to elevate men by an interest higher, deeper, wider than that of ordinary life.

In a simple sort of way, most corporations have a faith; most employees, if driven back to their basic beliefs and prejudices, would say that they thought they were doing something useful and worthwhile in this general sense, that they were helping increase the health or comfort or happiness or richness of the lives of their fellow men by virtue of their work with the corporation, and that the corporation was in general a force for good rather than harm in society. The great difference lies in the extent to which this personal feeling is exploited as the basis for the corporation religion.

Some corporations are extremely religious. They hold regular revivalist meetings at which rousing hymns are sung to the glory of the corporation and its products, and sales representatives are encouraged to stand up and give passionate personal testimony about why they believe. There is a trenchant sermon from the preacher (the senior executive present) and a hate session against the devil, the leading competitor. At the other end of the scale (which is also likely to be the other side of the Atlantic), the corporation regards religious observance as a personal and private matter and is only concerned that its staff should be believers in a fairly liberal sense. But in between there is a wide variety of religious practice and forms of religious observance: christenings (drinks to meet a new recruit to the department), funerals (farewell dinner, with speech sermons, to retiring executive), regular services for corporate worship (departmental or regional or area meetings, with pep-talk sermon from the manager reaffirming points of faith or doctrine where there are signs of divergence or laxity), communion (meetings for senior management only, in which highly confidential facts from the board are passed to the confirmed but kept from the rest of the congregation), and from time to time convocation, when the top men from all over the world come together. Corporations that would never go to the extremes of hymn singing and emotional personal testimony may yet contain much stronger religious feeling and observances than is apparent from the outside.

One reason why this is necessary is to fight heresy. Nearly all corporations operate on certain working beliefs that cannot be proved, which is another way to describe faith. Newspapers have such beliefs about their readers ("They want to be cheered up" or "They're not interested in a story that can't be told in 300 words"); shopkeepers, about their customers ("They'll always pay more for quality"); doctors, about their patients ("What they really come for is reassurance"); and all corporations, whether they are aware of it or not, have a number of such basic assumptions on which their success is founded. If these assumptions start to be questioned, then the roots of the corporation are threatened; and a group of young executives who started to act on different assumptions could destroy the whole concern. If a chain textile store built its reputation and success on the assumption that people really wanted durable, quality clothes, then a group who asserted that on the contrary they really wanted cheap clothes they could throw away after a month or two would undermine all the expertness, all the practices, all the training, all the customer loyalty and supplier standards built up over generations. For that reason the faith must be asserted and enforced. In corporation religions as in others, the heretic must be cast out not because of the probability that he is wrong but because of the possibility that he is right.

Doctrine, of course, is another matter; you can argue about doctrine. It is not axiomatic and fundamental, it has to do with practicalities, the best ways of achieving the objectives which have been determined in the light of faith.

The same chain store might say as a point of doctrine that sales staff should always stress the durable, lasting qualities of the clothes they sold; but if it became apparent that this put customers off, that they did not like the idea of wearing the same dress for four years, then the doctrine could be changed. So long as the faith was upheld, so long as the quality remained high, it would be possible to stress the cut and color and other fashion points and play down the durability, just as the Christian church has varied the emphasis of its message over the centuries from the fear of hell to the love of God without altering the creed or rewriting the Bible.

But a religion needs more than faith and doctrine and corporate worship; it also needs a supreme being. It is the role the creative leader is cut out for. If he is successful over a long period of time, divinity will start to hedge him. Many corporations have, or have had, such a leader, to whom his own staff and employees have attributed mystical qualities. This charisma is not a quality born in the leader, it is constructed for him out of the need for an object of worship and reverence, which exists in his staff coupled with the desire that the object of this worship should protect them from harm. Many leaders play up to it, and help to build their own myth. Montgomery was well aware that the glamorous publicity he received was a direct contribution to the high morale of the Eighth Army, but few corporations seem to realize the importance of a single, "divine" leader to the morale and religious fervor of their staff. Of course it has dangers too, but they are usually outweighed by the advantages. The point was once put to me with extreme perspicuity by the late Dunduza Chisiza, one of Dr. Hastings Banda's ministers in Malawi:

> All that our people can comprehend [he said] is a tribal chief. Therefore Banda must be a tribal chief and the

rest of us no more than a council of elders, at least in their eyes. Malawi must be built round him and identified with him. All national feeling must center on him, all decisions must be represented as his. This means that we are creating, by building this Banda King-figure, something we cannot destroy. Moreover by making him a figure of adulation and worship, we increase the danger of his believing in his own myth. If this makes him intolerable, we are still stuck with the image we have created.

He also added that it would be wise not to underestimate the need for such a single leader-figure among the so-called civilized people of the West. To quote Bagehot again,[2] where he talks of the need for a sovereign even though the cabinet is the instrument of government:

The best reason why Monarchy is a strong government is, that it is an intelligible government. The mass of mankind understand it, and they hardly anywhere in the world understand any other. It is often said that men are ruled by their imaginations; but it would be truer to say they are governed by the weakness of their imaginations. The nature of a constitution, the action of an assembly, the play of parties, the unseen formation of a guiding opinion, are complex facts, difficult to know and easy to mistake. But the action of a single will, the fiat of a single mind, are easy ideas: anybody can make them out, and no one can ever forget them.

Not all corporations, of course, have a leader to whom divinity could be attached with even a remote appearance of credibility. All the same, a little success and the right sort of internal publicity can work wonders. Other corporations are too vast; but there is no reason why the head of Cadillac should not be put over to the Cadillac division as their divinity, rather than the president of General Motors. The priests of Apollo do not deny the divinity of Zeus. It is, incidentally, a question who the priests are: I suspect they are the personnel officers, exercising their care of souls and holding occasional confessionals with the faithful who have reached a spiritual crisis about whether they are in the right department or moving up fast enough, and who confide to them domestic problems and anxieties that they would never admit in front of their closer colleagues. Compared with their counterparts in the Christian church, the corporation priests still have a lot to learn.

The strength of religion is never equal throughout the land: There are always some areas, some classes, who need it more than others. In industry it is the sales force whose need is greatest. They go out on their own among the heathen, they are the corporation missionaries. Other members of the corporation see only each other—it is easy to be a good Catholic in the Vatican. But the salesman travels alone to a spiritual Limpopo with only the strength of his faith to sustain him. He meets men who laugh at his god and deride his priests with tales of missed delivery dates and unmet specifications. Indeed, selling is very close to religious conversion: Before you can start selling your own product, you have to convince the prospect that there is something wrong with his present state, that he is missing something marvelous or heading for disaster. Only when you have created real internal disquiet can you start to sell your goods or gods.

Also, for all that may be said about figures and facts and performance and specifications, there is still a strong emotional, irrational element in most purchases. Not just of detergents and deodorants, but—so the salesmen tell me—of computers and machine tools as well. And for this, the salesman's own shining faith can be an important factor in tipping the balance. That is why he so desperately needs to sell himself first—his belief is actually an important part of the product. He is in the position of Sir Thomas More:

Whereas Galileo could recant, More could not; Galileo knew that whatever he said or signed, the earth would continue to orbit the sun, but More knew that his faith and martyrdom actually increased the strength of the Catholic Church. A salesman looking at a doubtful new product is like a priest receiving a new ruling on contraception, or a Communist confronted with a change in the party line on China: There is a tremendously powerful need to believe, even though the intellect may resist. After all, it is likely to put the salesman in a very sensitive position: He must be loyal to the firm that pays him, and yet very often the man to whom he will have to sell this new product has become, over the years, a personal friend. If he has an urgent command to push this product, which he knows is not right for his friend, what should he do? He is in the classic dilemma. It is no good saying that the long-term interest of his firm will not be served by selling a customer the wrong product—unless he sells it, the firm may have no future at all.

However, it can be done: Frederick Durrenmatt's parable play, *The Visit*, shows most persuasively how the offer of a million dollars or so enables the citizens of a small village to convince themselves that all considerations of ethics, morality, and common sense demand that they should—against their private, personal, selfish wishes, of course—strangle to death a man who had previously been the most popular person in the village. In the same way, the overriding need and desire to believe can usually compel belief against the protests of the intellect. The argument goes, "I may think it is a false doctrine (or crazy decision, or dud machine), but that is only my judgment. Am I going to be so arrogant as to set my unworthy judgment against that of all my superiors and the old man himself? And even if I am right, the cause, the faith, the firm needs the help of my belief to tide it over this difficulty, so that it can live on to fight for an object that transcends any single error. So I surrender my personal will to the overriding cause." It can be done, but the faith must be strong to compel it.

The other characteristic of most religions is a concept of ultimate reward and punishment, which can be used to compel good conduct by hope or fear. The industrial religion also has a hereafter, but it starts at sixty or sixty-five instead of death. The promise of a comfortable, reasonably affluent retirement is the hope; the threat of nothing except a few dollars of savings and the old age pension is the fear. The pension scheme is often the instrument through which these hopes and fears are operated, the silver cord that binds the employee to his firm ever tighter as he gets older. His early hopes and dreams fade, gradually he realizes he is not going to climb as high as he once hoped, and retirement on a comfortable pension becomes the only real goal to aim for. "If you work for Procter & Gamble for ten years," said one of their former executives, "you wonder if you can afford to leave."[3] The fear of losing the pension becomes ever stronger as time passes, as the afterlife gets nearer and fewer years of this one have to be endured. The fear of being fired is more than anything the fear of losing the pension, built up over so many years with such care, and without which the heaven of a comfortable bungalow with a garden by the sea becomes the hell of an old people's home. Before the comparatively recent idea of a retiring age, death was the only point after which anything nice could conceivably happen. Now it is sixty or sixty-five. And fortunately for those still working, their retired colleagues, whom they visit (once) on a day trip to Sun City, always say that everything is terrific—to say anything else would be to admit that all those years had been wasted. And so the idea of a Valhalla persists. Just occasionally one of them will come back, ghostlike, to the old firm, revisiting the glimpses of the moon, and say he is bored and unhappy and only wishes he could come back and take his coat off and get down to work again. His haunted colleagues, obscurely troubled, will try and exorcise him with jocularity ("Nonsense, Charlie, you're having a whale of a time; we know!") but they never take the hint about the job. He discovers that Omar Khayyám was right:

> And those that husbanded the golden grain
> And those who flung it to the winds like rain
> Alike to no such aureate earth are turned
> As, buried once, men want dug up again.

Perhaps, at those farewell parties for retiring executives, his colleagues who subscribe so generously to the presentation watch or tankard should fork out a little bit extra for a bell, book, and candle—just to be on the safe side.

# 26

## NONCONFORMISM

The state religion is by no means always the only religion in a country. A conquered population, for instance, will often keep its own religion despite efforts to impose on them the gods of its victors: Taken-over firms have been known to do the same. Equally, a variant religion can develop at the lower level of a society, especially if the society is stratified and it is difficult to rise socially from the lower to the upper level. The development of nonconformism in England was a social as much as a religious phenomenon: Church and chapel were respectively upper-middle class and lower class. When you realize that, however great your talents, you can never cross the social barrier, then you are ready to listen to a seductive preacher who offers an alternative to the church that both exemplifies and reinforces the repressive social system: Where the state religion glorifies opulence, he dignifies austerity; where the state religion has many orders of priesthood working closely with the political establishment, he emphasizes simply the independent preacher and his flock; where the state religion has rich lands and buildings, he offers a small, poor chapel built by the offerings of the faithful alone; where the state religion emphasizes God the Protector of the nation, he emphasizes Christ the Savior of the individual; where the state religion offers a place at the back of the congregation, he opens up all the offices of the church to any who wish to serve.

In the religion of the corporations, it is the labor unionists who are the nonconformists, the shop stewards who are the preachers, the conveners who are the bishops, and the national officers who are the rest of the spare, hardworked, low-paid hierarchy. The more rigid the two-tier structure of the company, and the more infrequent the promotions from the shop floor to management, then the stronger the nonconformist faith. Where the corporation religion sanctifies personal competition and graduated seniority, the union nonconformism exalts solidarity and equality; where the corporation religion has many grades of personnel officer working closely with management, the union emphasizes simply the independent shop steward and his members; where the corporation religion lays out lavishly for recreational and welfare facilities, the union offers a small room and a poor organization financed solely from members' dues; where the corporation religion emphasizes the continued profitability of the organization, the union emphasizes the continued increase of the paycheck; where the corporation religion offers only a place on the production line, the union throws open all its offices to any members who care to stand for them.

The "union problem," like the nonconformist problem, obviously cannot be solved until the social situation that bred it is changed. The difficulty, managements are inclined to say, is that segregation happens at school, and that all the best people from whatever social class become graduates and are recruited for management in their twenties, while those who come onto the production line in their teens are not of management caliber. This, I suspect, is to confuse the yogi with the commissar. Educational qualifications are evidence of yogi qualities only, and while not many of the high-powered yogis slip through the net, the commissars are presumably distributed more or less evenly between graduates and nongraduates. You do not have to go on listing the Walter Reuthers and Ernest Bevins to prove that men with great leadership qualities can arise from the unions. Many more extremely able men obviously remain within them, and are not considered for management posts because at some stage it was discovered that they only rated four out of ten as yogis, even though they may have rated nine or ten out of ten as commissars.[1] Since many managements are now finding that it is good commissars rather than good yogis that they are short of, there is perhaps a gleam of hope that this Figaro situation may one day be resolved.

There is another reason for hope as well. The English may yet learn to apply industrially the art they have practiced with such success politically: the art of assimilation. For centuries they have used it to avoid bloody revolution, and to preserve their royal family and institutions of privilege while these tumbled everywhere else. The English upper class have always had a genius for knowing when to give in to pressure from below, to let the steam rise before it blows the lid off. (The spectacular exception, Charles I, who did indeed get his lid blown off, is not in fact an exception at all. He was an unsympathetic and unyielding outsider.) The point is that revolt against a class system is never quite what it seems or quite what it believes itself to be. It usually thinks it is a revolt against injustice or political privilege or excessive taxation, but these are only the intellectual justifications of a more profound emotion. And the emotion is caused by social insult: The inherent social insult of an entrenched upper class that they can never belong to is so galling and humiliating to the best people of the lower class that they are prepared to do anything—storm the Bastille or the Winter Palace if necessary—to rid themselves of it. So the British upper class has had the wisdom to avoid trench warfare in the class struggle, to make tactical withdrawals wherever necessary. They yield by accepting into their own ranks the actual people who feel the social insult most strongly. John Burns and Ernie Bevin and J.H. Thomas, Ramsay MacDonald and Lloyd George, Walter Citrine and Bill Carron—if there seems a danger that they may knock the castle down, then the portcullis is raised, the drawbridge is lowered, and they can have what they want: cabinet posts, knighthoods, earldoms, premierships, everything. The upper-class men admit them to their clubs and the upper-class ladies to their beds. They are allowed to carry their reforms, if only they will trade in their desire to overturn the system. And since they are now part of the system, they trade it in willingly. Indeed, its only unforgivable fault was that it excluded them; now that it has reformed that, the rest somehow ceases to matter, and all is forgiven.

In the same way, there is a strong element of social rebellion behind the nonconformism of the labor unions. It may express itself in terms of wages and conditions, but the heat is generated by a more profound resentment. Sweden, which has never had a substantial upper-middle-class or rigid social stratification, has also one of the best worker-management relationships in Europe. Like all Western nations, they worship the same god, Growth; but they have avoided the British Schism, whereby management worship Him at the altar of profits and labor at the altar of wages. Only assimilation, I suspect, can start the necessary ecumenical movement in industry. There is no future for the archbishop in proclaiming that all are equal in the eyes of God if it is abundantly clear to three-quarters of the congregation that they are not equal to the other quarter in the eyes of the church. Only when their own members go to the theological college, become priests and bishops, and return to tell them that the luxury and idleness of the clergy are less than they used to believe, and the problems greater than they thought, do they start to believe it: because the man who tells them so is one of them. Equally, there is no future for the chairman in proclaiming that all are equal partners in the struggle for growth if it is abundantly clear to three-quarters of the corporation that they are not equal to the other quarter in the eyes of the board. Only when their own members start to be as simulated, to go to business school, become managers and executives, and return to tell them that the selfishness and incompetence of the management are less than they believed and the problems greater than they thought, do they start to believe it: again, because the man who tells them so is one of them.

This is not to suggest that once assimilation begins, bargaining will stop. Everyone's relationship with the corporation—shareholders', executives', employees'—rests on a contract that they can terminate at will, and that they may attempt to renegotiate from time to time either individually or collectively. But bargaining between members of the same church is very different from interdenominational negotiations. In the latter, both sides have the comfort that in the event of breakdown they will keep their precious independence; in the former, they have the fear that they may lose their even more precious unity.

# 27

## THE PRINCIPLE OF SELF-INTEREST

You might think that if you hire people, give them a guarantee of employment, a fair salary, and a well-defined job, you can assume from then onward that they will work for the good of the corporation that is employing them. Perhaps there are some who do. But on the whole it is safer to assume that, while the good of the corporation will always be an important consideration, it will not be their first loyalty: That is reserved for themselves, for their present status and rewards and their future career. And it is only too possible for their personal objectives to come into conflict with those of the corporation.

A firm that pays its department heads according to the number of staff in their department, for instance, is obviously tempting them all to increase their staff at every possible opportunity, and yet there are firms that do, in practice, use this as a salary yardstick without any such intention of helping solve the national unemployment problem. On the other hand the converse of this—some scheme like paying managers 10 percent of the salary of every post they abolish, so long as they continue to meet their targets—is almost unheard of, although just as logical. (Then again, in the 1990s economy, with so many layoffs and cutbacks, it may not be so unheard of after all.) Another example is firms that give the responsibility for authorizing new projects to someone who will get the blame if it fails, whereas someone else will get the credit if it succeeds. It is a system designed to squash all originality, enterprise, and daring. If, on the other hand, the one who gets the blame will also get the credit, they have a chance. British television offers instances of both systems: the BBC, which has the reputation for enterprise, experiment, and risk-taking, censors its own programs and takes the credit for the good ones and the blame for the bad ones; whereas the commercial companies, who have the reputation of being unenterprising and playing for safety, have to submit their programs to the Independent Television Authority. The authority gets no credit for any of the good programs, but a storm of abuse if it lets through any that are offensive, politically unbalanced, or in bad taste. It is not surprising if this causes a paralysis of the nerve. Or take the case of the man who is left in the same job for a long time, and realizes that he is never going to get much further—and say the job is advertising manager. He will make many friends in the advertising agencies, and his status among them will rise or fall depending upon the size of his firm's advertising appropriation. He will soon feel the temptation to get advertising appropriation increased to the utmost limit, not for the firm's good but for his own status with the agencies—quite apart from any considerations of what Santa Claus might put into his stocking.

The principle at the root of this is in fact the one outlined by Bentham as the basis of his political theory: The self-interest of individuals must be harnessed to the good of the state, or the corporation. It is easy enough at the lower levels, when you can simply say that the more productive a worker is, the better the corporation is served. In the same way, sales representatives' bonuses and commissions are constructed with painstaking and elaborate ingenuity to encourage them to sell hardest the goods that the company is most anxious to get rid of. But at the higher managerial levels it can be very difficult, as it becomes progressively easier for people to invert the process, to pursue their own interests while deftly harnessing the good of the corporation to them by subtle sophistries. By all means assume that any given manager is always working exclusively for the general good of the whole corporation, but construct the system so that he is penalized if he is not.

To arrange the internal structure of the corporation so that every manager's ego is pulling at full power in exactly the direction the corporation wants to go is quite an achievement. Even so, it is not enough: it produces high efficiency, but not necessarily internal unity. For that, every group's influence must be in proportion to its importance; formal representation must run along the lines of real power, power as it is now and not as it was, historically, when the institutions of state—the departments and committees and boards—were first set up. The new growth area of the organization—say, the photocopier group of a photographic firm, the automated technology group of a machine tool manufacturer—not only needs pay and encouragement in proportion to its success, it also needs political power, it needs its voice to be heard in the highest councils of the realm. It will have criticisms and grievances that need airing—usually about excessive budget, status, and too much importance given to less-booming but longer-entrenched departments, and insufficient attention given and respect given to its own aspirations and ideas—and if they are not heard and met, or at least satisfactorily answered, they are liable to turn inward in resentment, revolt, and even secession: It is a reformation situation. It happened in England in the nineteenth century, when the political power lay, as the constituency boundaries were drawn, with the rural landowning classes, whereas more and more of the nation's prosperity depended on the urban manufacturing and industrial classes. Not surprisingly, they felt that they were contributing so much to the nation's wealth and greatness, they should have proportionate say in how it was employed. The great battles over the Reform Bill and the repeal of the Corn Laws were a symptom of influence and importance being out of line: The unreformed parliament gave disproportionate weight to the countryside as against the towns, to the landowner against the industrialist, and the Corn Laws were seen as protecting the income of the unproductive landowning minority at the expense of dearer bread (and therefore a need for higher wages) for the laboring urban majority. The Reform Act of 1832 was the acknowledgment of the arrival of the new political force; the repeal of the Corn Laws in 1846 was proof of its strength.

The chief difficulty is that it is often only in retrospect that the ultimate importance of a growing group can be gauged. At the time, you do not know it is going to get any bigger, you suspect that improved competitive products will halt its progress or that it is just coming up to a plateau where demand levels out, in which case promotion and status raising could prove only an embarrassment. One of the first lessons of authority is that it is ten times easier to withhold than to withdraw. Political privileges, legal rights, welfare benefits—a state could hold these back from its people for many years; but once granted, taking them away is to risk a revolution. It is quite easy to refrain from making a section into a department or a department into a division; whereas to reduce a division to a department or a department to a section is an act of bureaucratic violence. The cell structure, of course, makes it much easier; so does the Hyman principle (Chapter 22) of having no titles, since Mr. Jones can continue to be Mr. Jones without trouble, whereas the controller of the administration division cannot be reduced to head of the administration department without personal anguish, and the desire to avoid such anguish may obstruct a necessary reorganization.

The problem of downgrading or removing an honest, loyal, and hard-working executive is always a thorny one: Logic cries out for it, nature rebels against it. You can say to the man, "You have done good and faithful service, your value is great, but this is not the job for you," and he may even believe you, but he knows all his colleagues and subordinates will know he has been pushed into a back seat. Many states have found a solution, or a partial solution, in an honors system. A peerage, a knighthood, an order of the legion of honor, or (under Louis XIV) the privilege of handing the sovereign his breeches at the levee, these are ways of demonstrating to everyone that this man remains in high personal esteem with the government, even though he has been passed over, removed, or downgraded in terms of function.

And the honors can also be used lower down the scale as a mark of favor for a rising young courtier who cannot yet be given the seniority his talents deserve. It is fascinating to watch the honors system developing inside the corporations: the development of a mass of small privileges and distinctions that of themselves convey no extra authority, carry no extra salary, and involve no extra function, and yet are avidly sought and jealously guarded by nearly all the executives. Titles (manager, executive, vice-president, director) are the obvious one—to be allowed to use a better-sounding title gives as much kick as a raise. Size of office is another; so is quality of furnishings; then there is the authority to order a tray of tea or coffee in the office, and the quality of the china when it arrives. There are the orders of dining (factory canteen, staff restaurant, senior managers' mess, board dining room) and parking (general parking lot, reserved parking structure, board parking spaces) and a wealth of other distinctions that start with name on door, and progress through secretary in separate office to the higher distinctions like bar and personal chauffeur. But although the system has developed with such wealth and complexity, most corporations are very shy about exploiting it. They tend to make these privileges the automatic accompaniment of certain levels of job, and to be slightly sheepish about their principles of segregation. But the time must soon come when the whole system is seen not as an invidious chore of the personnel department but, as it has been in so many states, a powerful weapon in the hand of the chief executive.

Then these distinctions, while still automatic at certain levels, can be awarded below that level for special incentive, reward, or compensation. Then the letter of rejection can read, "Dear John, I am afraid I have to tell you that we have finally decided we must award the vacant directorship to George Williams. Everyone agreed that you too are of director caliber, and amply deserve the seat on the board, but the final decision went his way. As you know, we cannot create another seat for you, but we hope you will lunch with us in the board dining room, and use all the other facilities reserved for directors, including the personal chauffeur service." It may not avert the blow, but it can soften it.

Of course the award must be seen to be the personal wish of the chief executive and not the impersonal decision of a committee; and, of course, it must not be asked to do too much, to act as the equivalent of promotion, as an adequate substitute for a raise. It is a lubricant, not a fuel. But if the corporation is going to make frequent mechanical adjustments to keep the weight of men's opinions in proportion to the weight of their responsibilities, then without regular lubrication there is liable to be constant friction and a great deal too much heat generated.

# 28

## DEMOCRACY AND THE CORPORATION STATE

Technically, democracy is a form of government in which ultimate power rests with the governed. Or something. If you try to define it more closely you get more and more involved, and when you try to clear your mind by going back to Athens where it all began, you find the whole system was supported by a vast voteless slave population and you give up in despair. So let us leave it at that. But, in a popular sense, "democratic" means something else; an attitude, an instinct, a way of doing things, which consults people in advance and takes account of their views and wishes and ideas before making final decisions. The former, technical democracy, the democracy of the ballot box, is sometimes called psephocracy, and because I want to treat them separately here, I will keep the distinction.

Democracy, the instinct and the attitude, is part of one of the oldest principles of good government, the principle of the two assemblies. The first is a small, powerful elite, which applies a high intelligence to the formulation of plans; the second is a large, popular, representative body, which applies its common sense to the consideration of the plans put forward by the first. The Greeks had the Boule and the Ecclesia, the Romans had the Senate and the Plebs, Britain once had the Lords and Commons and now has the Cabinet and Parliament, Bismarck instituted the Bundesrat and the Reichstag, the United States has the Administration and Congress. The idea is simple and obvious: Plans and policies and laws have a much better chance of succeeding if they are tested out in advance on those whom they will affect and who will have to execute them. The second assembly does not devise policy; it says, "Yes, our district will pay this tax for the navy because we are all sick to death of trade losses because of the maraudings of the pirates" or "No, the new land laws are so unpopular already that the magistrates just won't enforce any more." It says, "If you impose the tax on wheat, they will all just go and buy oats or imported rice. Why don't you put it on salt, where there is no alternative?"

Sometimes it volunteers information about unrest or discontent, or vents particular grievances, which can be dealt with before they turn into revolt. A democratic first assembly listens to all this, modifies its plans, dresses them up more attractively, and rides the planks of its policy along the waves of national feeling. And when the members of the second assembly return to their towns and cities, they are prepared to help make the laws work because they feel involved in the making of them. And having heard the arguments of the first assembly, they can explain to their fellows why this tax or this law is necessary, and why it is an improvement on the alternatives, and how it was they who suggested to the king that this was a fairer way and he agreed.

One of the best examples of this kind of democracy is the Bas-Rhone scheme in the South of France. Philippe Lamour, a farmer and former lawyer, read about the Tennessee Valley Authority and suddenly saw that exactly the same principle could be applied to his Languedoc: The hydroelectric power of the Rhone could pump its own waters over thousands of acres of near-wilderness, and transform a barren land into the orchard of Europe. It took years of surveys and negotiations, but finally he got the French government to agree to it, and to put up a large sum of money. That was all first-assembly work. There was, however, also the problem of convincing the highly conservative peasants that they would benefit, and here he acted on true democratic principles. He first irrigated his own farm at his own expense, just to prove to them how fertile the land could be, and he took parties of them over it to see the incredible sight of strawberries and melons growing on Languedoc soil. Then he talked, endlessly, to find their difficulties and objections, and some of them were considerable; especially the problem of landholdings—most were tiny and separate, the product of centuries of small deals and small bequests, whereas irrigation needed large single-crop areas. Then he outlined the overall increased profitability that irrigation would bring to each community, and left peasant conservatism to slog it out against peasant greed. But he never imposed any solution. He said to each area, "You come to me with your scheme, how you propose to redistribute the holdings, how much effort and money you are going to put into it, and then I'll judge it. If it's good, you'll get the irrigation supply in six months. If not, it will go to areas that have better schemes. It's up to you." The bureaucrat would have sent instructions, drawn up principles for priorities, tried to force legislation to alter the landholding laws, made regulations for the locating of pumps, issued standards for equipment and quotas for produce, and probably ended up with a giant white elephant. Lamour, an instinctive democrat, knew that the only hope was to sell his scheme, not impose it, and that the only people who could work out the local practicalities were the ones who would be affected by them and have to operate them; his democracy happens day after day over café tables, not once every five years in a polling booth.

Few chief executives could spend the time or summon up the patience of a Lamour. But his is, deliberately, an extreme case; the principle is simply that policy should be tested out on those who will be affected by it, and the details worked out by those who will have to implement it.

Alfred Sloan, when he took over General Motors, formed two assemblies: the executive committee, where policy was formed, and which contained no one from the divisions where the cars were made; and the operations committee, containing all the general managers of the divisions as well as the executive committee, not for policy making but for testing policy proposals, discussing the need for policy, and for making sure the two groups met each other regularly and listened to each others' suggestions and criticisms. The executive committee, in fact, served the classic function of the first assembly; and the operations committee, of the second. Almost all corporations have a first assembly—indeed survival without one is probably impossible—but by no means all of them understand the importance of the second; just as some corporations are more religious than others, so some are more democratic. The others, however, do not say, "We are undemocratic." They say, "We have an internal communications problem." All too often the man who says he has the communications problem actually is the communications problem: His transmitter is always going full blast, and he never switches over to his receiver.

This kind of two-assembly democracy can work extremely well within the framework of a monarchy, and produce a contented and well-governed nation. Its limitation, of course, is that if the king is weak or wicked and the barons cruel and oppressive, the second assembly can do nothing about it. However, as the level of wealth rises and its spread widens, the king becomes dependent on more and more of his subjects for taxes to run the kingdom. Then, on the principle of no taxation without representation, democracy becomes psephocracy, and those who contribute the money demand the right to vote on the method of spending it.

It is interesting to watch the growth of psephocracy in the corporations. They usually start as monarchies, with all the voting shares owned by the family, but gradually they need more capital and raise it from the market. Sometimes they contrive to issue nonvoting shares, and thereby keep control: As with states, so long as they govern wisely and well there is little complaint, and some great corporations still keep voting control in the family today. But more often the bulk shareholders want representation before they agree to put up large sums, and the monarchical power of the family is broken. At first it may only be one or two people, banks, or larger firms perhaps, who come in, but as time passes the level of wealth rises, and spreads, and more and more people join the electorate. The most powerful outside forces are the insurance companies and pension funds, who are beginning to insist on voting shares before they invest their thousands of millions in the corporations, and in a devious way this is a kind of universal suffrage. Almost everyone is insured in some way—life, pension, fire, car, accident, theft—and the millions of small premiums are like votes, with the insurance companies acting as parliamentary representatives not to formulate policy but to safeguard honesty, efficiency, and the good of the shareholders against incompetent or irresponsible management, and, if necessary, to vote the government out by voting the directors off the board. And so even if the employee has no vote as an employee, he may by virtue of being an insurance premium payer have a small part in bringing down the board if it is inefficient.

The managers, of course, are on to this, just as the politicians were. Bismarck and Disraeli both saw that to keep themselves securely in power the best way was to widen the franchise. A narrow franchise favored the well-informed liberals, who could force them out; a wide one enabled them to play on the simple, elemental hopes and fears of the ill-informed masses. Most managers of big corporations aim at the widest possible distribution of shares, and the maximum possible financing from retained capital, so that no well-informed block shareholder has a chance of producing a combination strong enough to remove them. So long as they provide a reasonable growth rate, the ill-informed, incurious, and inexpert shareholder will happily let things go on—which is one of the chief reasons why growth has become part of the national economic religion. If they fail, there may be a takeover bid, when a rival company makes a direct offer to shareholders—the nearest thing in corporation politics to an opposition fighting the government in a general election.

It is, of course, naked power politics, not party representation; but even this seems possible now. Some British trade unions are buying shares in corporations where they have a large membership, in order to make their voices heard at the annual meetings. So far, they cannot invest enough to have a sizable vote, but that might happen one day. Suppose, for instance, workers could designate a portion of their national insurance to be invested in the equity of the company employing them. After ten years, a labor-intensive corporation might find that its employees were a significant political force at the annual meeting. There is, however, another way, not so widely understood, by which the bulk of a corporation's labor force can achieve a kind of representation, and can influence decisions, at the highest level, and that is by the transition—already happening in some corporations—from casual labor to established staff. It is rather like the effect of the second Reform Act in Britain in 1867; by enfranchising not merely the substantial middle class—which happened in 1832—but also a huge mass of artisans, the government virtually transferred them from casual labor to staff. By giving them a political voice, the government guaranteed that in the future the chief hopes and fears of the working class would always be an ingredient in the formulation of policy by both political parties. In the same way, when a corporation transfers a sizable chunk of its work force to the staff, with the consequent guarantee of employment all the year round, it is implicitly guaranteeing that the provision of a full year's work for the section so enfranchised will be a built-in part of all future production planning.

There is another modern political development that seems to have its counterpart in the corporations: the rise of the nation-state. The difference is that it is happening the other way round. In the nineteenth century, the linguistic, cultural, national groups already existed, and the popular movement was to shake off the yoke of government by an alien culture and let each group govern itself: let Poland be governed by Poles, and not carved up among the Hohenzollern, Romanov, and Habsburg families, and so on. In the inverted nationalism of the corporations, the effort comes from above, to try to make the employees feel they are part of a social and cultural unit and not just working for a paycheck. The football and basketball teams, the photography club and the dramatic society, the dances and sports days and transatlantic charter flights for all the family, the house magazine and the weekly newsletter—all these are moves toward the corporation state. So far the corporations

have been weak on art, as compared with the nation builders of history, as an instrument for forging national pride.
Augustus employed Virgil to write a history of the firm's
early days, but few of the corporation histories are commissioned from authors of comparable distinction. Augustus
built a new city of marble, because he knew the value of
splendid architecture in creating a national spirit. So does
Pirelli the famous Italian tire manufacturer; and its employees, who work in one of the most famous modern
buildings in the world, cannot avoid a little nationalist
pride, as they read about it in foreign magazines, which is
denied those whose firms inhabit rectangular slabs identical to a thousand others. The empire builders paid artists
and poets to glorify the empire in beautiful pictures and
immortal words; the corporations pay advertising agencies
for copy and graphics to help sell their goods and enhance
their prestige. There have been some notable exceptions,
some distinguished paintings and films commissioned by
the corporations, but not on a scale with their power and
their wealth. However, it could happen yet.

The corporations even have their own political phi-
losophers, and the question, "What is the purpose of a
corporation?" is much canvassed nowadays. Is it to secure
maximum return on invested capital? Is it to ensure survival as a profitable enterprise? Is it to look after the welfare
of its employees? Is it to serve the nation? What, in fact, is
a corporation? The question is as unanswerable as "What
is a state?" a much older question, and for the same reason:
It is the same question, and there is no single answer.
Obviously a firm must stay profitable, just as a state must
stay unconquered, but the fact that it started simply in
order to make money does not mean that it must continue
simply trying to make money. England started as a merger
for the purpose of fighting the Danes, but she does not have

to go on fighting them indefinitely. Once the organization exists, corporation or state, it is for those who compose it to wield what power they can within it to make it the sort of organization they want it to be. They may want the dynastic paternalism of Nordstrom, the near-legendary retailer, the benevolent autocracy of the Walt Disney Company, or the reach-me-down democracy of the wholesale cooperative, and what they get will be the result of the interplay of uncontrollable external forces with the minds and wills of the men and women who as shareholders, directors, executives, and employees make up the corporation. This does not mean that the question "What is the purpose of a corporation?" is not worth asking, only that there is no correct answer. The utilitarian will say, "It is an agreement between a group of people to band together for the creation of wealth, which they then share out, the amount each receives being in proportion to the amount of his contribution to its creation"; the Hegelian will say, "The corporation is a concept, an idea, with an existence that is more than the people who from time to time compose it and the products it manufactures. Their duty is to serve it and to accept gratefully what they receive in return, and to pass it on stronger and even more glorious to those who follow them." You can say that either explanation is rubbish, but you cannot prove either is wrong. The question "What is *our* corporation for?" is another matter; you can hope not only to answer it but to change or modify the answer if you do not like it.

Another interesting question is the future role of governments. The paradoxical effect of the hydrogen bomb has been to remove war as an instrument of policy. This is not to say that some lunatic may not yet blow the world to bits; only that war is no longer a familiar sanction that can be credibly threatened or implied in diplomatic negotiations between advanced states. This, of course, does not stop nation competing with nation, it only makes the basically economic nature of the competition more visible and more important as nations compete by means of exports instead of armies. Is the nation-firm going to succeed the nation-state as the prime political unit? Management, says Drucker, is the setting of targets; was Britain's National Plan the first sign of the cabinet's transition from Her Majesty's government to the Board of U.K. (Holdings), Ltd., entrusted with the welding together and running of a vast production and trading enterprise? If so, they have a long way to go. Already the American government— U.S.A. (Holdings), Inc.—sees a great part of its role as boosting its own industries, and helping them directly in their competition with industries of other nations. NATO has been to them—among other things—a sales organization, and they have often used their political power within it to force the purchase of American equipment on their allies. Equally, their foreign policy of not giving strategic goods to Cold War countries was used to promote the sale of obsolescent American computers by trying to prohibit (for "strategic" reasons) the sale of new European ones.

In this new economic war, Britain is in danger of economic colonization by America and Japan. Neocolonialism is usually talked about by African states, but it happens in Britain too. Old colonialism exploited the raw materials, new colonialism exploits productive capacity and skilled management and labor; both take a high level of profit out of the colony and leave just enough wealth behind to make it worth the colony's while. The result of losing a colonial war is to watch your major productive corporations being taken over by corporations from the other country, and sending the profit back to the colonizer, and to see other corporations manufacturing their products under license and paying a heavy royalty. Then your best young people, the most inventive and original and enterprising and skillful, start to leave for the country where the pay is much higher and the most exciting work is being done with the best facilities, and you end up, metaphorically speaking, exporting watchmakers instead of watches. Then they lend you money to help you out, and you find the loan becomes a lever to control your foreign policy and your defense policy. Where African colonies look to pan-Africanism as a solution, Britain looks to pan-Europeanism, but with no real confidence that the last state will not be worse than the first. The hard realities of economic warfare and economic colonialism are only now becoming apparent; even so, if they turn out to be a substitute for military power politics and shooting wars, perhaps they are something to be grateful for. There cannot be much doubt that nowadays it is better to lose an economic war than win a military one.

There is, however, another possibility, namely, that the economic nationalism of governments may be defeated by the economic internationalism of the corporations. The corporation has perhaps not yet come to loom larger than the nation itself in the feelings of employees: Volkswagen employees in Germany feel that they are Germans more strongly than that they are Volkswagen people, General Motors men in Detroit are Americans first and GM people second, and so on. But there are signs that the corporation is creeping up: One of them is the increasingly international character of corporations. There was a point in Bismarck's career when his loyalty began to evolve and to change its object; from being the Prussian prime minister bent on acquiring German states to aggrandize Prussia he became, after their acquisition, a German first and a Prussian second: Prussia was a part of Germany, and an important part, but in Bismarck's mind her claims were weighed impartially with the claims of other German states that together with Prussia composed the German nation. There is some evidence that the boards of the corporations are beginning to think like Bismarck. "We think of ourselves, not as an American company with overseas interests, but as an international company whose headquarters happen to be in the United States," said the head of a large United States chemical corporation;[1] and he seems to have been speaking for a growing number of the international giants. As this process continues, there is liable to be wider and wider divergence between the corporation and the government, and the government cannot go on winning the loyalty tug-of-war forever. One day soon what's good for General Motors may be great for West Germany and South Africa, but disastrous for America.

# 29

## CONCLUSION

The realization that corporations and states are essentially the same organism opens up a broad territory, and I am conscious that having wandered into it more or less by accident I have come out with only a sketch map and a handful of traveler's tales. To those who complain of the omissions and inaccuracies that are inevitable in sketch maps, I can only say that it is still possible for professional cartographers to undertake a full and detailed survey if they are interested in the place; for one as unqualified as myself, the only alternative to a sketch map was nothing at all. Or, to change the metaphor, they can regard this as a software package, a computer program with a few sample runs, enabling anyone who is interested to hold his knowledge of history in file storage and run the data of his own corporation experience through the central processor of his mind and come out with his own results. It is the method and the approach that are important, not the conclusions.

More important still, perhaps, is the need for more historical data, for a reinterpretation of history. Each generation asks different questions of its historians: How can we avoid another world war, another slump, another Hitler? Why did the last one happen? What *did* happen? If the historians do not try to answer these questions directly, at least they write with the knowledge that their readers are interested in such problems, they have a sense of their audience. Today in the corporations there is a large unsatisfied audience: men and women with close personal experience of the politics of corporate organizations, of the wise and the weak and the sensible and the stupid and the tolerant and the tyrannical people who exercise power within them; of the internal tensions, the external struggles, the problems of organizing for war or creating a stable, smooth-running system to operate in peacetime. If they do not read much history, part of the reason is that so little of it is written with them in mind. Perhaps the new generation of historians will supply the omission.

There is another need for historians, too. Most of the management discussion has been conducted at too low a level: the level of systems analysis and work study and cost accountancy. Not surprisingly, some universities are slightly ashamed to include it in their curriculum. And yet the management of great corporations can be a dramatic, even an epic, subject, worthy of the most serious and detailed attention of the best minds in the country. It has been known for some time that corporations are social institutions with customs and taboos, status groupings and pecking orders, and many sociologists and social scientists have studied and written about them as such. But they are also political institutions, autocratic and democratic, peaceful and warlike, liberal and paternalistic, and only in the light of political history can that aspect of them be studied properly. The lower slopes can be explored by the schools of business management and the higher ones by the faculties of social science: to reach the peaks demands the training, the equipment, and the mettle of the historian.

The importance of a subject is often, in reality, no more than a reflection of the quality of mind brought to bear on it: A history of the world (if written by the wrong person) can be trivial and boring, a history of a local parish church (if written by the right one) can be a penetrating and absorbing account of England's transition from the Middle Ages to modern times. If management study is regarded as academically trivial and unworthy, the fault does not lie in the nature of management, but in the nature of the study. If this book has done no more than cut a small channel to link the rising lake of management theory with the broad ocean of history, and let the waters of each flow into the other, then it has done all that was hoped for it.

# ENDNOTES

**Chapter 2**

1. Richard Austin Smith, *Corporations in Crisis* (New York: Anchor, 1966), p. 119.

**Chapter 4**

1. Quoted in *Management Today* (November 1966).

**Chapter 7**

1. A.J.P. Taylor, *The Hapsburg Monarchy* (London: Hamish Hamilton, Ltd., 1948), p. 58.

**Chapter 9**

1. Hugh Trevor-Roper, *The Rise of Christian Europe* (London: Thames and Hudson, 1965), p. 184.

2. Quoted in *Management Today* (June 1966).

**Chapter 10**

1. Arthur Koestler, *The Act of Creation* (London: Hutchinson & Co., Ltd., 1964).

2. *Romeo and Juliet*, V, iii.

3. Koestler, *The Act of Creation*, Book I, Chap. VI.

**Chapter 11**

1. Edgar Wind, *Art and Anarchy* (London: Faber and Faber, 1963), Chap. VI.

2. John Kenneth Galbraith, *The Affluent Society* (London: Hamish Hamilton, Ltd., 1958). Chap. XI, "The Dependence Effect."

3. Vance Packard, *The Waste Makers* (New York: David McKay Co., Inc., 1960).

Chapter 14

1. H.B. Maynard, ed., *Top Management Handbook* (New York: McGraw-Hill, 1960), Chap. IX.

Chapter 15

1. Arthur J. Marder, *From Dreadnought to Scapa Flow*, 3 Vols. (Oxford: Oxford University Press, 1961), Vol. I, Chap. II.

Chapter 16

1. *King Henry the Fifth*, IV, i.

2. *Tamburlaine the Great*, Pt. I, l. 758.

3. *The Faerie Queen*, V, 2, 43.

4. Basil Collier, *The Battle of Britain* (London: Batsford, 1962).

5. Osman, Orkhan, Murad, 1299-1389.

6. Henry VII, 1485-1509; Henry VIII, 1509-1547; Elizabeth I, 1558-1603.

Chapter 17

1. Peter Drucker, *The Practice of Management* (New York: Harper & Row, 1964), Chap. X.

Chapter 18

1. A.P. Wavell, *Other Men's Flowers* (London: Penguin Books, 1960), p. 97.

2. Shakespeare, *Henry IV, Part I*, I, iii.

Chapter 19

1. Edward Gibbon, *The Decline and Fall of the Roman Empire* (London: J. M. Dent & Sons Ltd., 1910), p. 76.

2. Walter Bagehot, *The English Constitution* (London: Collins, 1963), p. 79.

Chapter 20

    1. Hugh Trevor-Roper, *Historical Essays* (London: Macmillan & Co., Ltd., 1963), Chap. X. Also see G.R. Elton, *The Tudor Revolution in Government: Administrative Changes in the Reign of Henry VIII* (Cambridge: Cambridge University Press, 1953).

Chapter 21

    1. Conversation with the author.

Chapter 22

    1. Bertrand Russell, *Freedom and Organisation 1814-1914* (London: George Allen & Unwin Ltd., 1934), p. 299.

Chapter 23

    1. Walter Bagehot, *The English Constitution* (London: Collins, 1963), p. 140.

Chapter 24

    1. Rudyard Kipling, "If."

    2. James Graham, Marquis of Montrose, "My Dear and Only Love."

    3. S.J. Simon, *Why You Lose At Bridge* (London: Nicholson & Watson, 1945), p. 11.

Chapter 25

    1. Walter Bagehot, *The English Constitution* (London: Collins, 1963), p. 63.

    2. Bagehot, *English Constitution*, p. 82.

    3. Vance Packard, *The Pyramid Climbers* (New York: McGraw-Hill. 1962), Chap. I.

Chapter 26

    1. Yogi-commissar rating is an entertaining and instructive game. You can play it with historical characters (Alexander: y-6, c-10; Talleyrand: y-10, c-2), or with your colleagues and superiors in the corporation. Preferably in their absence.

Chapter 28

    1. Geoffrey Owen, *Industry in the USA*, Chap. VIII.

# NOTES TOWARD A BIBLIOGRAPHY

## I. General

Burnham, James. *The Managerial Revolution*. Bloomington, Indiana: Indiana University Press, 1960.

*Discourses on the First Ten Books of Livy: The Discourses of Niccolo Machiavelli*, translated by Leslie J. Walker. London: Routledge and Kegan Paul, 1950.

Drucker, Peter. *The Concept of the Corporation*. New York: The New American Library of World Literature, Inc., 1964.

—. *The Practice of Management*. New York: Harper & Row, 1964.

—. *Managing for Results*. New York: Harper & Row, 1964.

Falk, Roger. *The Business of Management*. London: Penguin Books, 1961.

Galbraith, John Kenneth. *The Affluent Society*. New York: Houghton Mifflin Company, 1958.

Machiavelli, Niccolo. *The Prince,* translated by W. K. Marriot. London: J. M. Dent & Sons Ltd., 1958.

Pollard, Sidney. *The Genesis of Modern Management*. Cambridge: Harvard University Press, 1965.

"The Reith Lectures," *The Listener,* published by the British Broadcasting Company. London: November 17 to December 22, 1966.

Whyte, William H. *The Organization Man*. New York: Simon & Schuster, 1956.

## II. American Corporations

Harrington, Alan. *Life in the Crystal Palace*. New York: Knopf, 1959.

Owen, Geoffrey. *Industry in the U.S.A.* Baltimore: Penguin Books, 1966.

Packard, Vance. *The Waste Makers*. New York: David McKay Co., Inc., 1960.

*The Pyramid Climbers.* New York: McGraw-Hill, 1962.

Shonfield, Andrew. *Modern Capitalism.* London: Oxford University Press, 1965.

Sloan, Alfred P. *My Years with General Motors.* New York: Doubleday & Company, 1964.

Smith, Richard Austin. *Corporations in Crisis.* New York: Doubleday & Company, 1964.

*The Status Seekers.* New York: David McKay Co., Inc., 1959.

## III. British Corporations

Malik, Rex. *What's Wrong with British Industry?* London: Penguin Books, 1964.

Political and Economic Planning Ltd. "Thrusters and Sleepers," by P.E.P. Report and George Allen & Unwin. London, 1965.

Shanks, Michael. *The Stagnant Society: A Warning.* London: Penguin Books, 1961.

# INDEX

## A

Alexander the Great, 174
Ancient Greece, 68, 174
Ancient Rome, 7, 68, 72-74,
    143-144, 176, 206-208, 217
Antitrust laws, U.S., 55
Apple Computer, 16
Armada, 36, 53, 202

## B

Bacon, Sir Francis, 27-28
Bagehot, Walter, xii, 173, 201,
    219, 223
Barons
    money as weapon in war
        with corporation, 48-49
    role of, 161-163
    struggle between kings
        and, 41-48
Battle of Hastings, 25-26, 43,
    158
BBC Television Service, 69-70
Bevin, Ernest, 164, 231, 232
Bismarck, Otto von, 134-136,
    143, 188, 194-195, 213-214,
    217, 218, 248, 253-254
Bosses, managers vs., 142-143
British Army, 75-76
British Broadcasting
    Corporation (BBC)
    censorship by, 236
    management style within,
        7, 9-10
Burbage, Richard, 118

Burns, Thomas, 86
Butterfield, Herbert, 4, 26

## C

Caesar, Julius, 206-207
Caine, Michael, 195
Canon law, U.S., 55
Capitalists, 48
Carlson, Chester, 121-122
Carnegie, Andrew, 174
Carron, Bill, 232
Cell system, 84-90, 238
Centralization
    best form of, 73
    dangers of excessive, 67-68
    example of dilemmas
        faced regarding, 75
Change
    as concern of management,
        92-93
    related to technological
        advance, 99
    relationship between
        barons and courtiers due
        to, 165-166
    successors and, 170-171
Charles I (king of England),
    37
Chisiza, Dunduza, 222-223
Christianity
    decentralization and, 76
    meaning of medieval, 51-52
Chrysler, Walter, 65